Your Husband Your Friend

BOB BARNES

HARVEST HOUSE PUBLISHERS
Eugene, Oregon 97402

YOUR HUSBAND YOUR FRIEND
Copyright © 1993 by Harvest House Publishers
Eugene, Oregon 97402

Library of Congress Cataloging-in-Publication Data

Barnes, Bob, 1933-
   Your husband your friend / Bob Barnes.
       p. cm.
   Includes bibliographical references.
   ISBN 0-89081-959-9
   1. Marriage. 2. Marriage—Religious aspects—Christianity.
3. Wives—conduct of life. I. Title.
HQ734.B248   1993
306.81—dc20   92-46370
                                                                            CIP

Printed in the United States of America.

Dedication

This book is dedicated to my wife, Emilie, and to women like her who have stood by their husbands when they have felt like quitting.

You are an admirable group of women who will receive an extra reward in heaven. You have hung in there when there didn't seem to be any hope, when it seemed like just a matter of time before your marriage and family would break apart. Through it all, you trusted God, prayed with great fervor, and clung to that man you took in marriage. May we men become as committed to our marriage and family as you, our wives, are!

I thank God each day for the precious wife He has given me. I am the man I am today because of my God and my wife. Emilie has made this book possible. Without her, I never would have written these thoughts on paper.

Thank you, Emilie, for standing by me when you have felt like quitting!

Contents

Foreword

I met my Bob on a blind date. He said I was the date and he was blind, but I think we must both have been a little starry-eyed. I knew even then that he was the man I wanted to stand by for the rest of my life.

As with every marriage, there have been bumps in the road and times when we both felt like quitting. But we made a commitment on our wedding day. When the rough times came, we followed God's principles and stood with Christ . . . and we have never been sorry.

I want to encourage you: Stand by that man of yours! Yes, he will make mistakes. Yes, he may sometimes be insensitive. And perhaps you will too. But together you can make your marriage work.

The principles you are about to read are ones that have worked for us. Through these illustrations and insights you will discover why your precious husband may see life through a different lens than you and what you can do to better understand him.

My Bob and I have worked together professionally for many years. Each year we meet thousands of women just like you as we travel throughout the country. Bob has felt your heartbeat and is sensitive to your needs and desires for an intimate relationship with your husband. The message in this book comes from a man who loves God and wants to encourage us as wives to support and cherish and, yes, *stand by* our men.

Let my Bob touch your heart as he has mine.

Lovingly,

Emilie Barnes
Wife of a Great Man

A Personal Note from the Author

Did you look twice when you saw that a man wrote this book? Are you wondering, "Why does he think he can write a book of encouragement for women? Shouldn't a woman be writing this book? After all, she would know how hard it is to be a wife!" Those are valid questions, but now consider a different perspective.

Why do I think I can write a book of encouragement for women? Because, as a man, I know what a husband needs and wants from a wife! I know what makes a man feel loved and supported. I know what men need to feel confident and appreciated. I know the inner fears and questions a man lives with. I know the frustrations a man experiences in his various roles as breadwinner, disciplinarian, handyman, car repair expert, and spider killer. Simply put, I know how men tick—and that information can help you stand by your man. But there are other reasons why I believe I have an important message for you.

• I Have Been Schooled by a Wonderful Wife

For 37 years, I have been married to a woman who has truly stood by me. Emilie has shown me the patience of Job, the wisdom of Solomon, the forgiveness of Jesus, and the straightforwardness of Paul in her relationship to me. A very capable person in her own right and busy with her own areas of ministry, Emilie has always worked toward the long-term goal of helping me become the man God wants me to be.

Emilie has loved, encouraged, challenged, motivated, inspired, and supported me in every endeavor. She has stood by me, backing my ideas and my leadership even when she has had some doubts. When I have been wrong, Emilie has offered encouragement that next time would be different, not chastisement, scolding, "I told you so," or the silent treatment. For 37 years, I have been strengthened by her unwavering respect for me.

And for 37 years, Emilie has prayed for me daily. I know her prayers have changed the course of my life. Many times when I would kiss her goodbye as I left for work, I would mention my 10:30 A.M. meeting with the president of Company X or my 3:30 P.M. meeting with the staff. Then, at 10:30 and 3:30, I was confident that I had a faithful prayer warrior lifting me up before the Lord.

Through the years, Emilie's prayers have also put a protective hedge around my heart. Knowing that she would be in prayer for me has helped me realize that I can be protected from feelings of anger, resentment, defeat, or egotism. When I was away from the family at a convention, I knew that Emilie was praying for my safety, purity, obedience to God's Word, and protection from Satan's attacks. Also, being so in tune with God and with me, Emilie—like many intuitive wives—has often been aware of my needs before I've been aware of them myself. Finally, as a woman of prayer, Emilie is someone I can turn to with every decision that needs to be made, confident that her perspective will be godly and wise.

Emilie has also made me a hero to our children, Jennifer and Bradley. She has always made it a priority to teach them to support my leadership, appreciate me in word and deed, and respectfully acknowledge my role in the family. Just as Emilie has taught me what a gift a godly wife can be, she can undoubtedly teach you as I share from my experience as her husband.

• I Have Been Taught by God's Word

Through the years, I have studied the Bible—Old and New Testament alike—to see what God teaches men and women about marriage, children, and family. Even as a very young man, I wanted to mirror to the best of my ability God's principles for being a man, a husband, and a father. I truly want my life, my marriage, and my family to reflect what God teaches. While I'm still in the process of becoming all that God wants me to be as a person, husband, and father, I have tested the Bible's principles in the laboratory of life and found them to be sound. Now I can share what I have learned with you.

• I Have Listened to You

Since 1982, I have worked with Emilie in our "More Hours in My Day" ministry. During this time, I have listened to and spoken with hundreds of women across the country. Wherever Emilie and I go—California or New York, Texas or Michigan—women have the same concerns, questions, and desires for their man, their marriage, and their family.

- How can I get my husband to communicate with me?
- Why won't my husband share how he feels?
- What can I do to encourage my husband to be the leader in our family?
- How can I respect my husband?
- Why is he so involved in his job?
- Do men really have fragile egos?
- The children hardly know their father, and they don't understand him at all. How can I get the kids and their dad together?
- How do I love a husband who isn't a Christian?
- Are men really different from women?
- I know we loved each other when we were married, but I'm not sure we do now.
- What does a man want in a woman? In a wife?
- How can I make myself more attractive to my man?

I've heard you raise these issues and ask these questions—and I have some answers to share.

• I Know the Hope of the Lord

My heart is burdened by the many families I see who are separated and hurting because one or both spouses aren't willing to examine what God says about the sacred institution of marriage and come under the authority of biblical teaching. I am saddened by women I've seen who give up on their men too soon and make decisions about their marriage that are contrary to God's Word. At the same time, I am encouraged by what I've seen God do to revitalize marriages. I want to share the hope we have in Him with you who may be running low on hope for your marriage and family.

So why am I writing this book? Because I can offer you a unique and valuable look at marriage from a male perspective. I have learned much about marriage in my 37 years as a husband, and I have studied the scriptural guidelines and principles which God gives us as well. I have tested those principles and I trust them. I also know what you are concerned about, and I have hope in the grace of our Lord. I have seen Him bring new life to stale marriages, distant husbands, and weary wives. So hang in there! In the strength of the Lord and with the guidance of His Word, you can stand by your man!

Bob Barnes
Riverside, California

1

Facing the Challenge

By wisdom a house is built,
And by understanding it is established;
And by knowledge the rooms are filled
With all precious and pleasant riches.

Proverbs 24:3,4

Somewhere between the thrill of the engagement, the hectic preparation for the wedding, and the joy of The Big Day—and often despite excellent premarital counseling—the message gets lost, overlooked, or silenced. That message? Marriage is hard work.

Even in the best of circumstances, the demands of daily life and the hours one or both spouses work outside the home take their toll on the marriage relationship. Friends and lovers become business partners and virtual strangers. Children become the main topic of conversation and the primary focus of prayers. Older parents need care, bills need to be paid, the Sunday school program needs teachers, and the lawn needs mowing. Energy is gone long before the day is over— and the day is over long before the "to do" list is complete. Even with the Lord as the foundation, marriage is hard work.

The Way of the World

And marriage is made even harder these days by the world's view of men, women, marriage, and family. What the world preaches certainly isn't what God had in mind when He made us in His image, instituted marriage, and declared it good!

The Scriptures clearly teach that God created Eve from Adam's rib so that she could be Adam's helpmate (Genesis 2:18). Today's society, however, slams the door on that truth. Not wanting to be second-class citizens and mere helpers for the opposite sex, women have made some important and long overdue strides toward social, political, and economic equality, but as a result many have concluded, "Who needs men?" In response, men often become passive, quiet, and soft, quite unsure about their role as men. In fact, many men have no idea what God intends them to be, and women are frustrated because their men aren't meeting their needs in the marriage and the family. Women cry out to their husbands, "Get with the program!"— and the men softly ask, "What program?" Men and women alike have strayed from God's design for marriage and so are at odds with their mates.

Lies We Believe

Conflicts between husbands and wives are often triggered by certain ideas women in general have begun to believe about themselves and about men. In fact, clinical psychologist and author Dr. Toni Grant points out ten lies that the modern "liberated" woman has bought into, lies based on the false promises propagated by the more extreme elements of the feminist and sexual revolutions.[1]

• *You can have it all.* Society would have women believe that they can be high-powered CEOs, devoted wives, loving mothers, impeccable dressers, immaculate homemakers, gourmet chefs, creative hostesses, and disciplined exercisers. And women in pursuit of this impossible goal pay the price of a sense of failure, lack of fulfillment, and utter exhaustion when they don't live up to those unreachable standards. After all, as Dr. Grant points out, women—like men—are only human!

At our seminars, though, Emilie and I are seeing more and more Supermoms realizing that they can't have it all and deciding that they don't even want to try. In growing numbers, women are leaving the hard-charging corporate world and returning to the responsibilities, challenges, and comforts of home, children, and family—and they are content with their choice. They are realizing that they can't "have it all" and that they were paying too high a price in terms of their marriage, their children, their peace of mind, and their sanity, trying to achieve that illusory and impossible goal.

• *Men and women are fundamentally the same.* The idea that men and women are fundamentally the same has caused many women to adopt attributes and behaviors that run counter to their natural characteristics and temperaments. These women have been untrue to themselves as they have tried to be other than what God created them to be.

Clinical studies show consistently different play patterns between even young boys and girls, but we don't need sociologists and psychologists to point out the differences. Our own observation of the world around us and even limited contact with a member of the opposite sex reveal that men and women have different priorities, think different thoughts, and think differently—period. The basic differences between male and female (addressed throughout this book) are one reason why marriage is challenging and one fact which many women have denied in their quest for liberation and equality with their male counterparts. Let me say here that "different" does not imply better and worse, superior and inferior. And acknowledging that fact may help women be more comfortable being women—and not men!

• *Desirability is enhanced by accomplishment.* What makes a woman attractive to a man? Is it her keen business sense, her economic conquests in the corporate world, how many boards of directors she sits on, the number of postgraduate degrees she has earned, or the honors listed on her resumé? Does the power she attains by virtue of her many accomplishments win her the devotion of her man? Does love blossom where the woman has achieved much of what the world values in the way of status and success? No! Again, the world's lies have taken hold. This is not to say that women should not use their God-given gifts or strive to respond to God's call on their lives, but women are learning that their accomplishments don't necessarily win them a man's attention or devotion. Women are also learning that the top of the corporate ladder can be as lonely for them as it is for men.

• *Your full potential* must *be realized.* God calls each of us to use the talents and abilities He has given us, but too many of us have fallen victim to the idea that we have incredible potential and all of it must be realized. Few of us men and women are better than ordinary, and when we mere mortals strive for the stars, we will fail to reach them. Believing that we should always be able to win the gold medal or consistently score a perfect "10" can mean disappointment and depression when human limitations result in a bronze medal or an unexpected "8," "6," or even "2."

The Bible offers a message of freedom, though. Again and again throughout the pages of Scripture, we see how God uses ordinary people in His work. We don't have to be mental giants, well-trained scholars, or experts in the Bible. We need only to surrender ourselves to God and allow Him to do great things through us. Jesus teaches, "Whoever exalts himself shall be humbled; and whoever humbles himself shall be exalted" (Matthew 23:12). Resting on the truth of the Bible, we can be free from the myth of unrealized potential. Humbling ourselves before God yet willing to do our best wherever He calls us to work, we can let Him do what He will with our five loaves and two fish (Matthew 14:13-21).

• *Men and women view sex in the same way.* One basic difference between men and women is the way they approach and enjoy sex, and some of those differences are not hard to understand. First of all, the potential consequences of sexual intercourse—bearing a new life—have far greater ramifications in the life of a woman. Furthermore, the connection between sex and love is much closer and more important to women than it is to men, yet the sexual revolution has attempted to erase this difference. In their efforts to achieve equality with men, women have tried to ignore their fundamental emotional needs. Many sexually active women have sacrificed their souls based on the lie that they do or should approach sex just as men do. If women were to accept the fact that their Creator made them different from men, these women could again find wholeness, peace, and a more satisfying sexuality.

• *Motherhood can be postponed without penalty.* Quite often, women delay motherhood as they work toward career goals and, as a result, postpone marriage. Women ignore the fact that their reproductive system won't be able to reproduce forever. When they do suddenly hear the biological clock ticking, these women may panic. Their desperation for a child may then be heightened by any difficulty they have conceiving. Sadly, despite society's message to the contrary and today's high-tech medical advances, a woman's desire for children may never be fulfilled if she puts off motherhood too long.

• *Today's woman should abandon "softness" for "assertiveness."* The words *feminine* and *soft* no longer carry the positive associations they once did. In light of that fact, women choose assertiveness and strength—tools for the business world—over kindness, sensitivity, and compassion in their relationships. They don't seem to realize that attractiveness and real power come with such "feminine" characteristics. We men respond to women who are vulnerable and open to our love and care. Today, too many women wrongly equate such vulnerability with weakness. As we've seen before in this list of lies, women lose when they try to be like men.

• *Speaking one's mind is better than listening.* With wisdom that contrasts sharply to this popular modern myth, the New Testament writer James instructs believers to "be quick to hear, slow to speak" (1:19). In our culture which greatly values busyness, however, many of us—men and women alike—are more comfortable doing instead of being and speaking instead of listening. When women transfer their obsession to do and accomplish and achieve from the corporate world to the arena of male-female relationships, they often fail to be the kind of listener which appeals to a man. A more passive and receptive role, listening has been granted second-class status. As a result, men and women alike miss out on the bond which compassionate listening can forge between them.

• *A woman doesn't need a man except for breeding.* Remember the feminist rallying cry, "A woman needs a man like a fish needs a bicycle"? This slogan points to the myth of self-sufficiency, a myth which led Dr. Grant to label the modern woman "the Amazon woman." In the legendary Amazon culture, women functioned completely apart from men. Once a year, they would meet with men for breeding purposes, but they returned to their own island to raise the children.

This attitude that women don't need men is in direct opposition to the plan of our Creator. Men and women are to honor one another and lift each other up, and we honor one another when we humble ourselves. The writer of Proverbs observes that "a man's pride will bring him low, but a humble spirit will obtain honor" (29:23); Jesus teaches that "the greatest among you shall be your servant. And whoever exalts himself shall be humbled; and whoever humbles himself shall be exalted" (Matthew 23:11,12); and the apostle Peter exhorts his readers to "humble yourselves, therefore, under the mighty hand of God that He may exalt you at the proper time" (1 Peter 5:6)—teachings quite contrary to our society's prescriptions about success and to the myth that women can exalt themselves above men as people they simply don't need.

A more humble and biblical attitude toward one's spouse enables a Christian marriage relationship to reflect—as it should—the relationship between Jesus and His church. Just as Christ "loved the church and gave Himself up for her" (Ephesians 5:25), husbands and wives are to humble themselves in service to one another, and that doesn't leave much room for considering the opposite sex as necessary only for breeding! Furthermore, this godly marriage relationship is to be the foundation for raising children who will come to know, love, and serve the Lord. Many single parents today are doing their best to raise their children alone, but God's plan is to have husbands and wives be partners in this all-important and challenging task. The myth of feminine self-sufficiency sabotages God's design and runs counter to many biblical teachings.

• *A woman should look for sensitivity, not strength, in a man.* A softer, more sensitive man has not appealed to women the way people thought he would. While the new male sensitivity brings an important dimension to male-female relationships, women also want their men to be strong. So we men are left to figure out how to be strong but not obnoxiously macho, and sensitive without being weak. I hear many Christian men today wondering how to be both the man the Lord and the man their wife want them to be. Since we as a society have strayed so far from biblical principles, the way out of the grasp of this lie—and the other nine as well—is hardly clear.

Challenging the Lies

Consider again the litany of lies we've just looked at: Women can have it all, men and women are fundamentally the same, accomplishment means desirability, women must realize their full potential, men and women are alike in their attitudes and approach to sex, women can put off motherhood without penalty, women should be assertive instead of soft, speaking one's mind is better than listening, women don't need men, and women should look for sensitivity instead of strength in a man. Now consider the impact these lies can and do have on our society. What role have these widely accepted lies played in the harsh realities of families breaking up and teenagers being lost to drugs?

Believing in and acting on these lies not only undermines society, it also means living contrary to God's plan. When we try to change who God made men and women to be and redesign the plan He instituted in the beginning, our efforts dishonor the Creator. Despite that fact and despite their negative consequences, these lies still influence much of society's thinking about men and women. And speaking out against these lies and myths is not always well-received.

Remember when First Lady Barbara Bush addressed the women at Wellesley College? Her comments received harsh criticism from the all-women student body. But look again at what she said:

> At the end of your life, you will never regret not having passed one more test, not winning one more verdict, or not closing one more deal. You will regret time not spent with a husband, a child, a friend, or a parent.
>
> We are in a transitional period right now— fascinating and exhilarating times, learning to adjust to changes and the choices we—men and women—are facing. As an example, I remember what a friend said on hearing her husband

complain to his buddies that he had to babysit: Quickly setting him straight, my friend told her husband that when it's your own kids, it's not called babysitting.

Now, maybe we should adjust faster and maybe we should adjust slower. But whatever the era, whatever the times, one thing will never change: Fathers and mothers, if you have children, they must come first. You must read to your children, and you must hug your children, and you must love your children. Your success as a family, our success as a society, depends not on what happens in the White House but on what happens inside your house.[2]

Barbara Bush boldly spoke out against many of the lies women and men alike have fallen prey to. In doing so, she challenged women of all ages across America to evaluate the choices they are making and the impact those choices are having on American society. In effect, Mrs. Bush called women to deny the lies of the past two decades. And the teachings of the Bible—as we'll look at in this book—call you to do likewise. Will you respond to the call?

Standing by Your Man

On Mother's Day 1991, our local newspaper ran a story that speaks to our times. Letha Blacman recalled the time when, pregnant with her first child, she left her husband of two years and went home to Mother. For 30 minutes, she told her mother what she was unhappy about and that she was leaving her husband and their home—although when she wrote the article Letha couldn't remember why she was so angry with her husband!

When Letha stopped talking, her mother said this: "I have listened to you, and now I am going to tell you what you are going to do. You are expecting a child. It needs a mother and a father. You are going back to your husband, and the two of you are going to raise that child."

The next morning, Letha's husband went to her mother's house and took Letha home. Angry that her mother hadn't opened her arms and said, "Come home, honey," Letha didn't even wave goodbye as she and her husband drove away.

The punch line of the story? Letha and her husband raised that first child and a second as well. On April 23, 1991, they celebrated their fifty-ninth wedding anniversary.[3]

Letha stood by her man when she felt like quitting. She stood strong against the lies of society which would have encouraged her to make it on her own. And you can do the same.

You can stand by your man when you feel like quitting. You can stay at his side even when things are tough and the struggle is intense. With guidance from the lessons of this book and in reliance on God's strength, you can survive the difficult times and do so with patience, love, and hope.

2

Gaining a New Perspective and Finding Hope

If any of you lacks wisdom, he should ask God,
who gives generously to all without finding fault,
and it will be given to him.

James 1:5 NIV

Whenever I buy a new insurance policy, household appliance, or pair of jeans, I pay attention to the disclaimers:

- "It is agreed that no insurance shall be effective unless the applicant passes a complete medical examination."

- "This warranty is valid only if the product is used for the purpose for which it was designed. It does not cover products which have been damaged by negligence, misuse, or accident or which have been modified or repaired by unauthorized persons."

27

- "Wash and dry with like colors. Color may transfer when new. Wash before wearing. Shrinks approximately 10%."

We consumers live in a world of disclaimers. Manufacturers regularly provide guidelines for the use and care of their products and specifics about when they will and when they won't stand behind their work. Their instructions also keep consumers from having expectations that exceed what the item can deliver.

Early in this book, I also want to offer several disclaimers. Like today's manufacturers, I don't want you to expect more than a book like this can deliver, so I offer the following five points.

1. *Simple, surefire formulas don't exist.* I would love to be able to give each of you a white pill that would ease all your concerns and answer all your questions, but there aren't any such pills on the market. As much as we'd like an easy, clearly marked path out of the difficulties we face, not even in Scripture do we find three simple steps for avoiding or coping with life's challenges.

And life does bring challenges and questions that don't have simple answers:

- How can I have a good marriage?
- How can I be the kind of wife my husband wants to live with?
- How can I help my husband stop drinking?
- How can I keep my children drug-free?

There are no formulas for dealing with issues like these. What works for one person won't necessarily work for another; what works in one situation won't necessarily work in another.

Although it doesn't offer us pat formulas for living, God's Word does offer us guidelines for living the Christian life, building a Christian marriage, and raising children to know and love the Lord. In the chapters which follow, we'll look at these guidelines, trusting God to show you how to apply them in your specific circumstances. Again, there are no guarantees that your life will be free of pain, heartache, and disappointment, but you can find hope in God's love for you and the promise that He "causes all things to work together for good to those who love God" (Romans 8:28).

2. *Wives are not to be change agents.* Many people who say "I do" think that, after they are married, their spouse will change. But nowhere in Scripture does God appoint spouses to be change agents for one another.

Despite that fact, many women I meet at our seminars ask me how they can change their husbands. I gently remind them that the Holy Spirit—not the wife—is the change agent. Speaking to this same situation, Ruth Graham wisely says, "Tell your mate the positive, and tell God the negative." Talk to God about your marriage. Ask your heavenly Father to work change through His Spirit—and know that He may change you as well as your spouse! Also, focus your efforts on the role which Scripture clearly sets forth for you: "Be subject to one another in the fear of Christ. Wives, be subject to your own husbands, as to the Lord . . . and let the wife see to it that she respect her husband" (Ephesians 5:21,22,33). Women are not to seek to change their husbands. Women are called to honor their husbands out of honor for the Lord.

Likewise, men are not to seek to change their

wives, and I know from experience what results from such efforts. Whenever I've tried to change Emilie, I've provoked tension, discouragement, and resistance in her. Consider the fact that, as human beings, we have a strong tendency to do the opposite of what we are told to do. We want to touch wet paint when the sign says, "Wet Paint." Children want to test the "no" when we instruct them to stay away from matches, water, and friends we don't approve of. Likewise, our spouses will do the opposite of what we suggest when, usually through negative communication, we try to change them. Discouraged if not angered by our criticism, our spouse can come to resent our words and inwardly resolve, "I'll show him/her!" In such situations, we can actually hinder God's work in our mate's life. God, working through His Spirit, is to be the change agent. We can only hinder His work in the life of our spouse when we try to be helpful with criticism that is anything but constructive.

Through the years, God has also shown me that many times my responses to Emilie's shortcomings were worse than her shortcomings. I have found myself, for instance, becoming angry, unkind, resentful, and moody in the face of her shortcomings, and these responses were far worse for our relationship and my walk with the Lord than her shortcomings were. Even today I remember how negative I became when I tried to change her—but I honestly can't remember the specific shortcoming I was trying to correct! I do remember, though, coming across the teachings of Ephesians 4:29—"Let no unwholesome word proceed from your mouth, but only such a word as is good for edification according to the need of the moment, that it may give grace to those who hear." That verse led me to adopt "Is that edifying?" as a guideline for my speech, and that little question has been extremely helpful in keeping my words to Emilie positive.

Experience has also taught me that husbands and wives alike need to be sensitive to verbal and nonverbal messages to our spouses, and we need to ask forgiveness for our improper responses. Rather than making insensitive and inappropriate efforts to change our mates, we must support them in prayer and be willing to wait for the Holy Spirit to do His work in their lives.

Many women (and men) don't want to wait, and often self-centeredness is the main reason. Wives want their men to fit their ideals for the perfect husband—and to fit those ideals now! Are you one of those wives? Consider your attitude toward your husband in light of this instruction from Scripture: "Do nothing from selfishness or empty conceit, but with humility of mind let each of you regard one another as more important than himself; do not merely look out for your own personal interests, but also for the interests of others" (Philippians 2:3,4). We are to be subject to our mate out of fear or reverence for God, and we are to ask God to help us love our mate as He calls us to.

Put differently, instead of focusing on changing your mate, concentrate on what God wants from you. First Peter 3:1,2 tells women how to live with an unresponsive mate: "Wives, fit in with your husbands' plans; for then if they refuse to listen when you talk to them about the Lord, they will be won by your respectful, pure behavior. Your godly lives will speak to them better than any words" (TLB). Is this easy to do? Not until you accept the fact that God designed marriage relationships to work best according to His guidelines.

When both the husband and wife are submitted to

Jesus as their Lord and Savior, both will be living according to God's plans for marriage, and both will be open to the work of the Holy Spirit in their lives as individuals and in their life together. And, again, the Holy Spirit is the One who changes our spouses—and who changes us—to conform to the image of Christ. In light of that fact, this book is more a "how to love and pray for your spouse" than a "how to change your spouse" manual.

3. *Each of us carries baggage from childhood.* Today, the word "baggage" is used to describe more than the suitcases we carry when we travel. Today the word also refers to the behaviors, thought patterns, and deep-seated wounds we carry. This baggage weighs us down and keeps us from being the people God wants us to be. Not surprisingly, this often-hidden baggage also interferes with our relationships, keeps wives from knowing their husbands, and causes painful and frustrating conflicts in a marriage.

This book cannot free you from that baggage or heal the hurts from your past experiences. It can, however, remind you that your husband—like you—entered the relationship with some kind of baggage. It can also call you to confess any current baggage—the sin which also prevents us from being all that God wants us to be. Freeing yourself from baggage—past and present—will enable you to stand by your man.

4. *We are at war with the enemy.* As Paul writes in Ephesians 6: "Our struggle is not against flesh and blood, but against the rulers, against the powers, against the world forces of this darkness, against the spiritual forces of wickedness in the heavenly places" (v. 12). We believers truly are at war with Satan and his

army, and he would love to destroy your marriage. After all, good marriages are a testimony to God and His love. God wants us to have healthy relationships based in Him, but Satan wishes to confuse our lives so that we no longer know what is right. Your daily newspaper with its stories of murder, hatred, runaways, divorce, and death shows that Satan is alive and well and hard at work causing confusion and heartache in our world.

As part of his work, Satan the Deceiver may send a coworker, unsaved friend, or neighbor with advice for you. Weigh the advice to see if it meets the standards of Scripture. (Martin Luther says, "The best way to drive out the devil, if he will not yield to tests of Scriptures, is to jeer and flout him, for he cannot bear scorn.")[1] Keep in mind, too, that Satan can bring struggles and difficulty to your marriage, and his solution will be, "Run!" This book can't protect you from the battle with Satan, but this book can remind you that the Holy Spirit says, "Stay," and that the Holy Spirit will help you do just that (Ephesians 6:10-17).

5. *We are all sinners.* In Romans 3:23, the apostle Paul teaches that "all have sinned and fall short of the glory of God." As sinners, we are not perfect; all of us—wives as well as husbands—fall short of God's commands and our spouse's expectations. When your husband disappoints you, don't be surprised. Even though he is a believer who has been cleansed from his sin, he brings into your marriage—as you do—the sinful nature of human beings. Slaves to this sinful nature, all of us do things contrary to what we would like to do (Romans 7:15). As sinners, we hurt the very people we love. This book can't change your sin nature or your husband's. But this book can and will call you

to follow in the footsteps of Jesus and extend to your husband forgiveness, patience, and unconditional love.

Finding Hope in God's Grace

After reading all that this book can't deliver, are you discouraged? Such despair is common in our world today. The faces in the news and in our communities—the faces of people of all ages—reveal a lack of hope. This book can help replace that hopelessness with the hope of God that never disappoints.

And as Dr. Larry Crabb reminds his readers in his book *The Marriage Builder*, the hope of the Christian lies not in a change of circumstances which God may or may not bring about, but in the grace of God. We aren't to hope that our spouse will change, our business will turn around, or our children will straighten out. Instead, we are to hope in God's grace—in His unearned, undeserved, and unconditional love for us.

Larry Crabb writes this:

Remember that the Lord has not promised to put your marriage together for you. The hope of the Christian is not that one's spouse will change or that one's health will improve or that one's financial situation will become good. God does not promise to rearrange our worlds to suit our longings. He does promise to permit only those events that will further His purpose in our lives. Our responsibility is to respond to life's events in a manner intended to please the Lord, not to change our spouses into what we want.... Certainly if both partners build on the foundation of hope and strive earnestly to live biblically, even the worst marriage can be turned around. Either way, there is reason to hope. This reason is bound up in the truth of the grace of God.[2]

This call to rest in God's grace is one of the most important messages for the Christian church today. We need to realize that anything and everything we are going through in our marriage is the forge God is using to work in our life, not the life of our mate. God is dealing with you, and your relationship to Jesus Christ and how you honor that relationship within your marriage is to be your primary concern. As you focus on becoming the person God wants you to be, you will see and experience His grace in your life, and that grace will mean hope and perhaps even change in your marriage.

Take a moment right now to ask God what He is trying to teach you. Ask Him to show you what He is doing so that you can better understand and accept the challenges you are facing. You may not receive an immediate answer, but even pausing for prayer will give you a taste of the hope and the peace God has for you. Think back, too, on past times when you struggled to know what God was doing in your life. Looking back, do you see now how God was at work? Let that incident be a touchstone of faith that will encourage you to persevere today.

Removing Some Stumbling Blocks

I also encourage you to reevaluate your expectations for marriage. Everyone enters marriage with unrealistic or, at best, clouded expectations. These false ideas come from childhood dreams and popular novels, movies, and television programs, and these false ideas often result in what Dennis and Barbara Rainey term "the phantom husband." Did you think you were marrying the person described here?

He rises early, has a quiet time reading the Bible and praying, and then jogs several seven-minute miles. After breakfast with his family, he presents a fifteen-minute devotional. Never forgetting to hug and kiss his wife good-bye, he arrives at work ten minutes early. He is consistently patient with his co-workers, always content with his job, and has problem-solving techniques for every situation. At lunch he eats only perfectly healthful foods. His desk is never cluttered, and he is confidently in control. He arrives home on time every day and never turns down his boys when they want to play catch.

This phantom is well-read in world events, politics, key issues of our day, the Scriptures, and literary classics. He's a handyman around the house and loves to build things for his wife. He is socially popular and never tires of people or of helping them in time of need. He obeys all traffic laws and never speeds, even if he's late. He can quote large sections of Scripture in a single bound, has faith more powerful than a locomotive, and is faster than a speeding bullet in solving family conflicts. He never gets discouraged, never wants to quit, and always has the right words for every circumstance. He also keeps his garage neat. He never loses things, always flosses his teeth, and has no trouble with his weight. And he has time to fish.[3]

While the Raineys' words may have made you smile, they may also have opened your eyes to your unrealistic and unfair expectations for your husband. Although the world would lead you to believe that you can have it all in the way of the perfect career, a perfect home, perfect children, and the perfect husband, the Bible teaches otherwise. Jesus teaches that we will have trouble in this world—but that He overcomes that trouble (John 16:33). So don't let false expectations—that ideal and purely imaginary phantom husband—keep you from learning all that God wants to teach you and experiencing all that God has for you in your marriage.

Consider, too, the wisdom of the Hawaiians. A few years ago after doing a seminar in Honolulu, Emilie and I were taking a bus to the airport on a rainy Sunday morning. Commenting on the rain, the driver stated, "Today will be a celebration for some newlyweds." Looking out the window, I saw nothing but rain and couldn't understand the driver's words. I asked her, "What do you mean it will be a celebration?" She replied, "In Hawaii, we say that rain on your wedding day is cause to celebrate." I thought to myself, "In California, the rain wouldn't be a cause for celebration—it would be a disaster." We want and even demand perfection. Our Hawaiian counterparts, though, have learned to live with imperfection. Have you in your marriage?

Living with a Purpose

Imperfection in the world—in our homes, our spouse, and ourselves—is easier to live with when we are reaching for something greater than anything this world can offer. What are you reaching for? What is your purpose in life? What meaningful verse of Scripture does God seem to have given specifically to you as a statement of your purpose in life? If you haven't thought about this, why not start now? God's living Word does indeed have truth, guidance, and hope for you. Find a verse that will give you those things and let it be a purpose statement for your life.

Emilie and I have chosen Matthew 6:33 as our theme verse—"But seek first His kingdom and His righteousness; and all these things shall be added to you." In all of our decisions, Emilie and I ask the basic question, "Are we seeking first God's kingdom and His righteousness?" Through the years, this basic purpose statement has given us direction and purpose.

In her book *Survival for Busy Women*, Emilie explains how you can develop long- and short-range goals based on your purpose statement that will help you meet that purpose. When you have set forth specific goals that will help you fulfill your purpose in life, you can more easily determine your priorities. If certain activities or opportunities don't help you reach your goals for your life in general and your marriage in particular, you may want to say, "No, thank you." Say no to the good things in life and save your yeses for the best.

Living life with a purpose can change despair to hope, and hope will mean joy even when life is difficult. Living with a purpose rooted in God's truth will also help you experience more fully the grace of God which saved you and which can make you unselfish, humble, kind, considerate, patient, wise, and loving within as well as outside your marriage.

Surviving the "Tunnel of Chaos"

So you want to experience the hope of God's grace, remove from your marriage the stumbling blocks of unrealistic expectations and demands for perfection, and live with a purpose that is more important than the irritations of day-to-day life—but getting there seems too risky?

Author and pastor Bill Hybels shares with his readers some ideas about moving toward open, honest, and authentic relationships. Bill explains that the call to truth and authenticity must have greater value than simply maintaining peace in the relationship. This call to truth challenges us to address and resolve misunderstandings, share feelings, talk through offenses, and deal with doubts about each other's integrity. Hybels calls this experience "the tunnel of chaos." The tunnel of chaos is where "hurts are unburied, hostilities revealed, and tough questions asked." When misunderstandings are not resolved, relationships deteriorate. In Hybels' words, "The secret agendas of hurt and misunderstanding lead to detachment, distrust, and bitterness. Feelings of love begin to die. It's the story of too many marriages, family relationships, and friendships. . . . No matter how unpleasant the tunnel of chaos is, there's no other route to authentic relationships."[4]

When we truly want the peace that awaits on the other side of the tunnel and are willing to deal with the chaos in the tunnel, then we are ready to move ahead. The risks are real and the work is difficult, but the rewards of an authentic relationship are worth the treacherous journey through the tunnel. Inside the tunnel, explosions happen, rocks fall, lights go out, horns blow, and people shout—but what a beautiful sunlit morning awaits on the other side.

Are you standing at the mouth of the tunnel today, wanting what is on the other side but afraid to enter? Recall for a moment the wedding vows, those promises you made to your husband and to God. Being true to those vows will cost you (it costs everyone), but God's rewards for such obedience will be a great blessing. The tunnel may seem dark and its confusion and the battles that await you overwhelming, but I encourage you to take that first step. After all, how do you move a mountain? You pick up the first stone and get to work. How do you survive the tunnel of chaos? A step at a time—and that will get you to the other side.

3

Stand by Your God

I love the Lord because He hears my prayers and answers them. Because He bends down and listens, I will pray as long as I breathe!

Psalm 116:1,2 TLB

Perhaps you're surprised by the title of this chapter. Do you wonder what standing by God has to do with standing by your man? Let me assure you that the connection is vital. Nurturing your relationship to the Lord is crucial to being the kind of woman and wife He calls you to be.

Consider the fruit that comes from spending time with your heavenly Father. In Galatians 5, Paul writes that "the fruit of the Spirit is love, joy, peace, patience, kindness, goodness, faithfulness, gentleness, self-control" (vv. 22,23). Think about each item in that list.

How will each of those God-given qualities enable you to stand by your man? Which of us doesn't need a touch of God's love, patience, kindness, goodness, gentleness, and self-control in our marriage? Those are the things—as well as guidance, wisdom, hope, and a deeper knowledge of Him—that He wants to give to us His children.

Finding Time or Making Time?

"But," you say, "who has time? My 'to do' list is always longer than my day. I run from the time the alarm goes off every morning until I fall into bed at night. How can I possibly find time to do one more thing? When could I find even a few minutes to read the Bible or pray?"

I answer your questions with a question: Are you doing what's important in your day—or only what is urgent? Your relationship with Jesus Christ is the most important part of your life. Isn't that what your life verse—or your search for a life verse—tells you?

Let me also share a saying that is important to Emilie and me: "People do what they want to do." All of us make choices, and when we don't make time for God in our day, we are probably not making the best choices.

I also want to remind you that God greatly desires to spend time alone with you. After all, you are His child (John 1:12; Galatians 3:26). He created you, He loves you, and He gave His only Son for your salvation. Your heavenly Father wants to know you, and He wants you to know Him. The Creator of the universe wants to meet with us alone daily, and that daily communion with Him is indeed the best way to get to know Him. How can you and I say no to that opportunity?

So how can you get to know your heavenly Father? Simply by spending time alone with Him. There's not a single right time or one correct place. The only requirement for a rich time with God is your willing heart. Know that your meeting time with God will vary according to the season of your life and the schedules you are juggling in your home. Even Jesus' prayer times varied. He often slipped away to be alone in prayer (Luke 5:16). He prayed in the morning and late at night, on a hill and in the Upper Room (Mark 1:35; Luke 22:41-45; Matthew 14:23; John 17). Many men who spend a great deal of time driving on the California freeways use those times to be with God. Emilie used to get up earlier than the rest of the family for a quiet time of reading the Scripture and praying.

Much of my studying and preparing to teach a lesson serves as my quiet time with the Lord. Many times, though, I read God's Word and dwell upon His thoughts even when I don't have a lesson to prepare. And—maybe I'm one of the oddballs—I love it when we get to church early and I have 10 or 15 minutes to open my Bible and think upon God's thoughts. Despite the distracting talk that is often going on around me, I use this block of time to set my heart and prepare to worship. (In fact, I believe if more of the congregation devoted this time to reading Scripture and praying for the service, the pastor's messages would be better and church would be more meaningful for every worshiper.)

Again, the times and places where we meet God will vary, but the fact that we meet alone with God each day should be a constant in our life. After all, God has made it clear that He is interested in us who are His children (1 Peter 5:7).

Getting Started

So you want to spend time with God each day but aren't sure where to start? Open with a word of greeting. In a short prayer, ask God's blessing on your time together. A small group I was part of opened our morning meetings with a song, and you may want to greet God with a song, too. Don't worry if you don't have a good voice. God cares more about your heart!

Reading God's Word

After you greet the Lord, spend some time reading the Bible. Jesus teaches that we can't live by bread alone; we need God's Word to nourish and sustain us (Matthew 4:4). If you're not sure where to begin, I recommend starting with the gospel of John. If you're getting acquainted with the Bible for the first time, you'll find God's love for you beautifully explained and His plan for you carefully outlined in this book.

As you read the Bible, think about the words and meditate on them. "Meditating" simply means to think seriously about spiritual things. Think quietly, soberly, and deeply about God—about how wonderful He is, what blessings He has given you, and what He wants you to do. As you read and meditate, you may notice one or more of the following:

- A special promise you can claim
- A principle to help you in your daily life
- A command you should follow
- A light that reveals some sin in your life
- A meaningful verse that you'll want to memorize
- Comfort or insight for the hard times you're facing
- Guidance for the day ahead
- Hope that encourages you and that you can share with someone you care about

Don't read too quickly or try to cover too much material at one sitting. Take the time to look for all that God has specifically for you in the verses you read.

Spending Time in Prayer

After you've read and meditated on God's Word for a while, spend some time with God in prayer. Talk to Him as you would to your earthly parent or a special friend who loves you, desires the best for you, and wants to help you in every way possible.

Are you wondering what to talk to God about when you pray? Here are a few suggestions:

- *Praise* God for who He is, the Creator and Sustainer of the whole universe who is interested in each of us who are in His family (Psalm 150; Matthew 10:30).
- *Thank* God for all He has done for you . . . for all He is doing for you . . . and for all that He will do for you in the future (Philippians 4:6).
- *Confess* your sins. Tell God about the things you have done and said and thought for which you are sorry. He tells us in 1 John 1:9 that He is "faithful and righteous to forgive us our sins."
- *Pray* for your family . . . and for friends or neighbors who have needs, physical or spiritual. Ask God to work in the heart of someone you hope will come to know Jesus as Savior. Pray for our government officials, for your minister and church officers, for missionaries and other Christian servants (Philippians 2:4).
- *Pray*, too, for yourself. Ask for guidance for the day ahead. Ask God to help you do His will . . . and ask Him to arrange opportunities to serve Him throughout the day (Philippians 4:6).

Know that time with your heavenly Father is never wasted. If you spend time alone with God in the morning, you'll start your day refreshed and ready for whatever comes your way. If you spend time alone with Him in the evening, you'll go to sleep relaxed, resting in His care and ready for a new day to serve Him.

Remember, too, that you can talk to Him anytime and anywhere—in school, at work, on the freeway, at home—about anything. You don't have to make an appointment to ask Him for something you needed or to thank Him for something you have received from Him. God is interested in everything that happens to you.

Developing a Prayer Notebook

Devote yourselves to prayer, keeping alert
in it with an attitude of thanksgiving.
                                        Colossians 4:2

Like any other activity, your prayers will be more consistent when you are aware of answers to your prayers and when you approach your prayers in an organized way. In our "More Hours in Your Day" seminars, we suggest how you can easily manage this very important segment of your life by developing your own prayer notebook.[1] All you need is a three-ring binder (we recommend 8"x 5"), a set of tabs, and 100 sheets of lined paper that fit into your notebook. In your notebook, you'll keep track of prayer requests and have space for sermon outlines, notes, and any special verse or message God gives you.

1. First, label six tabs "Monday" through "Saturday" and insert several pieces of paper behind each divider.

2. Put sermon notes behind a "Sunday" tab or "Saturday" tab, depending upon your day of worship (see p. 59).

3. Use two more tabs for miscellaneous sections. These sections might include Bible study notes, a record of

your daily Bible readings, personal prayers, favorite Scriptures, a list of Scriptures you've memorized, personal goals, and even names, addresses, and phone numbers.

4. Now, on a separate piece of paper, make a list of prayer requests. You can use the following headings:

- **Family** (immediate and extended)
- **Personal** (your relationship with God, your role as homemaker, your weaknesses, your relationships with people, your goals, etc.)
- **Finances** (budgetary concerns, decisions about major purchases, investments, saving for retirement, home improvements, etc.)
- **Illness** (Great Grandma Gertie's hip, Aunt Barbara's lupus, your special friend's addiction, Bill's glaucoma, etc.)
- **Career** (challenges, decisions, etc.)
- **Government/Schools** (the President of the United States, state and city leaders, day-care centers, colleges, your local school board, your children's teachers, etc.)
- **Church** (your pastor, the staff, the youth, etc.)
- **Missions** (ministries and missions like Campus Crusade for Christ, Focus on the Family, Billy Graham, InterVarsity, Mission Fellowship, "More Hours in My Day," Navigators, Wycliffe Bible Translators, Young Life, Youth for Christ, the 700 Club, missionaries you know or know of)

5. Now decide which topics you'll pray about on which day of the week. Leave Sunday or your Sabbath for sermon notes. Your week may look like this:

Monday—Family (use one page for each member)
Tuesday—Church and Missions
Wednesday—Personal
Thursday—Finances and Career
Friday—Illness
Saturday/Sunday—Government/Schools

(At the top of each page, place a picture of the person or group for which you are praying. That image will make it easier for you to pray—and people will gladly provide a picture if they know you are praying for them.)

Your prayer notebook will help you organize your concerns, look for God's answers to your prayers, and note the words of encouragement and hope that God reveals to you in His Word. When Emilie hears of prayer needs, she first records them on her list of "Prayer Requests." Later she transfers them to the appropriate page and prays for that item at the same time she prays for similar concerns. She would, for instance, pray for Bevan's fever on Friday with other people fighting an illness (see p. 58).

As you keep track of what you want to pray for, your prayer life will be more satisfying than any hit-or-miss approach you may have used before. And as you keep a record of your prayer requests and God's answers, your prayer life will be very rewarding. You'll find your prayer life greatly enriching your Christian walk.

Filling a Prayer Basket

Even with a prayer notebook, Emilie soon realized that she could easily be discouraged about prayer time if she had to run around the house to get her Bible, a pencil, and her notebook. So she decided to use a medium-sized basket as her "prayer basket." In it, she places all of her tools for her appointment with God:

- Her prayer notebook
- A pencil or pen
- Her Bible
- Some tissue for when tears come
- A small bunch of fresh or silk flowers to remind her of God's love and of His Spirit
- And a few cheery note cards for writing a note of encouragement to a friend or relative[2]

If you have a prayer basket like Emilie's, you'll always be ready for a special meeting with Jesus. All you need now is a special spot to meet with Him. Depending on the time of year, you might sit by the fireplace with a cup of hot tea or by the lake with a glass of iced tea. Find a spot free of distractions and away from interruptions. Maybe it will be a favorite chair that you use only for this time with the Lord. That way, you'll know when you sit down in that chair that you're there to meet with God.

One more word about your prayer basket. Besides keeping you organized, it will serve as a concrete reminder of the time you want to spend alone with the Lord. If you haven't picked up your basket in a day or two, that little straw friend of yours will cry out as you pass and say, "Pick me up so we can spend time with Jesus!"

Create in Me a New Heart

As you begin to stand by your God and spend time with Him regularly, you will realize that, with your old heart, you can't do what is necessary to make you a godly person. In fact, none of us can make that transformation happen under our own power—and fortunately we don't have to. In Ezekiel 36:26, God says, "I will give you a new heart and put a new spirit in you." God offers us a heart transplant, one that is even more remarkable than the transplanting of physical hearts which has almost become commonplace.

Thankfully, not every one of us will need a new physical heart, but each one of us does need a spiritual heart transplant. Why? Because we are born with a sinful nature. King David acknowledges that fact in the psalms: "Behold, I was brought forth in iniquity, and in sin my mother conceived me" (51:5). The prophet Jeremiah writes, "The heart is deceitful above all things and beyond cure" (17:9). Jesus teaches that same lesson in the Gospels: "Out of the heart come evil thoughts, murders, adulteries, fornications, thefts, false witness, slanders (Matthew 15:19). The apostle Paul wrestles with his sin nature: "For the good that I wish, I do not do; but I practice the very evil that I do not wish. But if I am doing the very thing I do not wish, I am no longer the one doing it, but sin which dwells in me" (Romans 7:19,20). And the apostle John is very direct in his statement about sin: "If we say that we have no sin, we are deceiving ourselves, and the truth is not in us" (1 John 1:8).

So what are we to do? Not even the most skilled physician can cure a sinful heart or give us a new and pure one—but God can and, according to His promise, will. In *Seeing Yourself through God's Eyes*, June Hunt talks about this process:

> Slowly, after this divine transplant, healing begins and, as promised, your new heart becomes capable of perfect love. Your self-centeredness is now Christ-centeredness. There is healing to replace the hatred; there is a balm for the bitterness. You can face the world with a freedom and a future you have never known before.

"Create in me a clean heart, O God, and renew a steadfast spirit within me" (Psalm 51:10). Once you have a changed heart, you have a changed life. You can love the unlovable, be kind to the unkind, and forgive the unforgivable. All this because you have a new heart—you have God's heart![3]

This kind of heart operation, at the loving hands of your divine Physician, doesn't require major medical insurance. There are no disclaimers or deductibles. God offers this transformation to us free. It cost Him greatly as He gave His only Son for our salvation, but it's a gift to us. All we have to do is accept it—no strings attached.

A Prayer for All Seasons

As we spend time with God, we open ourselves to His work in our hearts and in our lives. Then, as we see Him working, we will want to know Him even more. We will want our prayer life to be all that it can be. What does that mean? How should we be praying?

In the Scripture, we find many models of prayer, and probably foremost among those prayers is the Lord's Prayer (Matthew 6:9-13). This wonderful example of a prayer includes important elements of prayer. We find words of adoration, of submission to God's will for our life, of petition, and, in closing, of praise. We can learn much from the model our Lord gave when His disciples said, "Teach us to pray" (Luke 11:1).

As meaningful as the Lord's Prayer is to me, I have also found Colossians 1:9-12 to be a powerful guide in my prayer life. If you aren't in the habit of praying or if you want to renew your time with God, I challenge you to read this passage of Scripture every day for 30 days. Look at it in small pieces, dwell on its message each day, take action upon what it says, and you'll become a new person.

Read how Paul and Timothy pray for the church at Colossae:

> We . . . ask that you may be filled with the knowledge of His will in all spiritual wisdom and understanding, so that you may walk in a manner worthy of the Lord, to please Him in all respects, bearing fruit in every good work and increasing in the knowledge of God; strengthened with all power, according to His glorious might, for the attaining of all stead-fastness and patience; joyously giving thanks to the Father, who has qualified us to share in the inheritance of the saints in light.

Now read the prayer again and think about what a wonderful prayer it is for you to pray for your husband and children. I know for a fact that Emilie has prayed for me every day of our marriage, and I am sorry that I cannot say that I have done the same for her. Knowing that Emilie is praying for me is a real source of encouragement and support. If you aren't praying for your husband daily, let me suggest that Colossians 1:9-12 be your model. Look at what you'll be asking God:

- That your husband will have the spiritual wisdom and understanding he needs to know God's will.
- That he will "walk in a manner worthy of the Lord, to please Him in all respects" (v. 10).
- That your husband will bear "fruit in all good work and increasing in the knowledge of God" (v. 10).

- That he will be "strengthened with all power ... for the attaining of all steadfastness and patience (v. 11).

You would then end your prayer by joyously giving thanks to God for all that He has given you—your husband being one of those gifts (v. 12).

Did you hear those words? What armor of protection and growth you can give your husband with a prayer like that! With these powerful words and the Lord at his side, your husband will be able to deal with the challenges he faces. I also encourage you to tell your husband that you are praying for him each day, and if he is receptive, tell him the specifics of your prayers for him. Let me assure you that it is a real comfort to have my wife praying for me, asking God to give me wisdom and understanding, to enable me to honor Him in all I do, to help me bear fruit for His kingdom, and to grant me strength, steadfastness, and patience.

Know, too, that these verses from Colossians are a good model for your prayers for other family members, your friends, your neighbors, and yourself as well as for your husband. After all, each one of God's people needs to know His will, honor Him in everything they do, grow in the knowledge of the Lord, and be strong, steadfast, and patient as we serve Him.

So You Want More?

When becoming a godly woman is a priority and you are spending regular time alone with your heavenly Father in prayer, you will see Him blessing you with the fruit of the Spirit. He will be filling your life more and more with "love, joy, peace, patience, kindness, goodness, faithfulness, gentleness, self-control" (Galatians 5:22,23). Your husband will notice these qualities, your children will wonder what's happening to Mom, and you will undoubtedly want to grow even closer to the Lord. How can you do that? Here are some suggestions.

• *Focus on Jesus Christ.* From the time you wake to the time you sleep, try to be aware of Jesus' presence with you. Emilie and I start each day with a word of inspiration taken from several devotional books or easel-type flip charts that we have. Among our favorites are Oswald Chambers' *My Utmost for His Highest,* H. Norman Wright's *Quiet Time for Couples,* and Charles J. Spurgeon's *Morning and Evening.* We then try to carry that word with us throughout the day to remind us of a certain truth about or promise from God. When you find a passage that is especially meaningful, don't be afraid to underline it, mark it with a brightly colored highlighter pen, or make notes in the margin. Books that are marked up like that become good friends along the walk of faith.

• *Study God's Word daily.* When you start the day with a devotional reading, you might come across a specific point or a key verse that you'd like to study in greater depth, and a chain reference Bible is excellent for this purpose. The Thompson Chain Reference Bible, for instance, is available in the King James and the New International Version (NIV) translations, and it has an excellent system of Bible study helps including an index and a reasonably complete concordance.

For your Bible study times, consider using a New King James Bible, the New American Standard Bible, or the New International Version with cross-references. Besides being written in modern English for easier reading and comprehension, these versions have margin notes and footnotes that direct you to other passages that are similar in content, thought, or words. Talk to the staff at your local Christian bookstore. They can help you choose the Bible that will serve you best.

One last note. The Living Bible doesn't have the extra features for study, but it is certainly a pleasure to read. We have one on our nightstand by the bed, and we often pick it up for its ease and clarity.

Whichever Bible you read and study, use your highlighter pen liberally. (Be sure to get the kind made especially for Bibles so the ink doesn't bleed through the paper.) Also take time to write your thoughts in the margins. You might, as I do, date a passage of Scripture when it has particular relevance to the circumstances of your life or the significance of your study. Comment on new understanding you gain in a familiar verse. When you do these things, the Bible becomes a much more personal guide and friend.

Rather than relying on your morning devotional reading to prompt you to read a section of Scripture, you may want more structure, and many different types and levels of Bible study guides are available. Again, the staff at your local Christian bookstore can recommend an appropriate starting point for your personal Bible study time.

Let me also encourage you to get involved in Bible Study Fellowship if there is one in your area. This international group sponsors community Bible studies for women and is known for its very competent leaders and excellent materials.

• *Write out your prayers.* Well-known authors Fred and Florence Littauer encourage their readers to spend 30 minutes or so in prayer after their time of daily Bible study. At first, Fred himself wondered what he would talk to God about for half an hour, but now he rarely prays for less than that.

What caused the change? Writing out his prayers word for word. Every day he opens his 8"x 11" spiral binder and writes until he's finished praying. He dates each entry and indicates what Scripture he studied that day. Fred writes:

> Praying has now become an indescribable blessing, never the "chore" that it sometimes was in the past. I cannot write fast enough to keep up with my thoughts, so there is never a lag. No longer am I sending up ten cent prayers and expecting million dollar answers! No longer does my mind wander, as it formerly did, when I am praying. No longer do I 'doze off' as has happened before, especially in the early morning.
>
> Instead of praying *to God*, I have found that I am often having communion *with God*. God has spoken to me clearly during these prayer times. . . . The writing of my prayers has also greatly deepened my love for the Lord, the sense of adoration I have for Him, my desire to praise Him at all times. Surely it has greatly strengthened my faith.[4]

Are you challenged by Fred's words? Intrigued by the possibility of having such a vital prayer life? Then why not try it? Writing out your prayers may become a real blessing instead of a chore, and it may strengthen your faith just as it has strengthened Fred's.

Keeping a Journal

As you write out your daily prayers, you'll notice that these prayers reflect how you feel about yourself, your husband, your children, and the circumstances of your life. You will become aware of feelings and ideas that have been hidden. Keeping track of these feelings and thoughts in a journal can be an excellent means of growing spiritually and personally.

Emilie also encourages women to keep a daily journal as they go through some very traumatic event in their lives, and many have written to say how much they appreciated the journal. Haven't you often thought, "I won't forget that thought/event/feeling" and later wish you'd written it down? If you keep a journal—during the smooth times as well as the rough times—you can look back at a particular time and recall all the vivid details as if it were yesterday.

Looking to God Each Day

Like the children of Israel who looked to God each day for food, we are to look to Him each day for spiritual nourishment as well as practical guidance. When we stand by our God and spend time alone with Him daily, we also find ourselves in a position to be richly blessed by our heavenly Father. He wants us, His children, to look to Him daily and to walk through each day aware of His presence. A regular time of devotional reading, Bible study, and prayer is essential to God's transforming work in our lives.

As H. Norman Wright points out, a regular quiet time also helps us live according to God's will, not our own: "The key to realizing the Holy Spirit's control is our will. If we are determined to do things our own way, we will continually struggle with God. We have a choice. We can live under the tyranny of our own thoughts, feelings, choices, and behaviors, or we can live under the control of the Holy Spirit. Think about it. Your choice will change your life."[4] And let me add that your choice to live under the control of the Holy Spirit could change your marriage! After all, it is God's Spirit which grants you the "love, joy, peace, patience, kindness, goodness, faithfulness, gentleness, self-control" that will enable you to stand by your man (Galatians 5:22,23).

Sample Prayer Page
Friday: Illness

Date	Request	Scripture	Update/answer	Date
1/1	Evelyn's mother's surgery	James 5:14	Successful	1/4
1/3	The Fields' baby	Heb. 4:16	Okay	1/24
1/22	Grandma's hospital stay		Out of hospital	1/29
1/23	Pastor Foor		Better	2/5
2/3	Bevan's fever	Col. 4:2	Gone	2/6
2/20	Phil Jackson's surgery		Still some pain—keep praying	3/1

Sermon Notes

Date: _May 4_ Speaker: _____
Title: _____ _Choose For Yourself_ _____
Text: _Joshua 24_ _____

Farewell address II —
A review of Israel's history

The pronoun "I" (God) is mentioned
    17 X's
Contrast between Israel & our growth
    A. History   vs. 4-5
    B. Birth of a Nation   vs. 6-7
    C. Growth & Adolescence   vs. 8-10
    D. Mature Manhood   vs. 11-12
    E. Obedience   vs. 13
    F. Call for a decision vs. 14-15
        (We all serve someone)
    G. Response of the people vs. 16-18
    H. Warning by Joshua   vs. 19-24
    I. Joshua makes a covenant
        with the people   vs. 25-28
    J. Joshua dies   v.s. 29

    What is my decision?
    Talents? Faith? Time?

4

Stand by Your Commitment to God and to Your Husband

How blessed is the man who has made the Lord his trust, and has not turned to the proud, nor to those who lapse into falsehood.

Psalm 40:4

You've probably never heard of Nicolai Pestretsov, but now you may never forget him.... He was 36 years old, a sergeant major in the Russian army stationed in Angola. His wife had traveled the long distance from home to visit her husband when, on an August day, South African military units entered the country in quest of black nationalist guerrillas taking sanctuary there. When the South Africans encountered the Russian soldiers, four people were killed and the rest of the Russians fled—except for Sergeant Major Pestretsov.

The South African troops captured Pestretsov, and a military communique explained the situation: "Sgt. Major Nicolai Pestretsov refused to leave the body of his slain wife, who was killed in the assault on the village. He went to the body of his wife and would not leave it, although she was dead."[1]

What a picture of commitment—and what a series of questions it raises. Robert Fulghum, the teller of the story, asks these questions:

> Why didn't he run and save his own hide? What made him go back? Is it possible that he loved her? Is it possible that he wanted to hold her in his arms one last time? Is it possible that he needed to cry and grieve? Is it possible that he felt the stupidity of war? Is it possible that he felt the injustice of fate? Is it possible that he thought of children, born or unborn? Is it possible that he didn't care what became of him now? Is it possible? We don't know. Or at least we don't know for certain. But we can guess. His actions answer.[2]

What do your actions say about your commitment to your husband? What do your attitudes and your words reveal about your commitment to your spouse? Standing by the commitment you made to your spouse—the commitment you made before God and many witnesses—is key to standing by your man.

Commitment to God—and to Your Spouse

Picture again Sergeant Major Pestretsov kneeling by the side of his wife's lifeless body. That level of commitment—not wanting to leave the woman to whom he'd pledged his life even when his very life was at stake—is a powerful illustration of Paul's words to husbands in Ephesus and husbands today: "Love your wives, just as Christ also loved the church and gave himself up for her" (Ephesians 5:25). We who are married are to be as committed to our spouse as Christ is committed to the church He died for. In fact, as Christians, our marriages are to be a witness to the world of Christ's love and grace. Clearly, marriage is not an institution to be entered into casually.

In light of the importance God places on marriage, Emilie and I take very seriously the premarital counseling we do. We never, for instance, encourage two people to get married if one is a Christian and the other is not (2 Corinthians 6:14). A marriage needs to be rooted in each partner's commitment to love and serve the Lord, or else the union will be divided from the start as the two people look in different directions. Besides, only a Christian marriage will result in a Christian home, and only a Christian home can glorify God and be the witness to the world which God calls His children to be.

As a young man, I had to wrestle with God's command not to marry an unbeliever. When I met Emilie, she was an unbeliever, and I knew I could not marry her. One night, as we sat on the sofa in her living room, I held Emilie's face in my two hands and said as firmly and lovingly as I could, "Emilie, I love you very much, but I can't ask you to marry me!"

Looking steadily into my eyes, she said quietly, "Why not?" My answer reflected the most important decision I ever made other than accepting Jesus Christ as my personal Savior. With all the courage I could muster, I said gently, "Because you are not a Christian!"

Emilie was shocked. She had seen me as the type of man she could love and eventually marry. In her innocence, she asked me, "How do I become a

Christian?" From that moment, she began to consider whether Jesus might actually be the Messiah that her Jewish people had long awaited.

After several months of seeking answers, she prayed one evening at her bedside, "Dear God, if you have a Son and if your Son is Jesus our Messiah, please reveal Him to me!" Emilie expected a voice to answer her immediately, but God waited a few weeks to reveal Himself to her. Then, one Sunday morning, Emilie responded to my pastor's challenge to accept Jesus Christ as her personal Savior, and that evening she was baptized.

As I look back over our 37 years of married life, I know without any doubt that if I had married a nonbeliever, my life would be very different. Being obedient to God has meant being blessed by a rich and wonderful marriage rooted in His love and dedicated to Him. Furthermore, vowing before God to love Emilie through the good times and the bad has reinforced my commitment to her when the times were indeed bad. Had my vows been to Emilie alone, they might have been easier to walk away from, but God's witness and the foundation He gives to Christian couples keeps us able to stand together whatever comes our way.

The Words of Commitment

Your story may not be a story of a happy, solid marriage or of complete obedience to God's Word. Instead, you may feel very much like quitting, whether you're married to a believer or a nonbeliever. Whatever the situation, let me remind you of the vows you made before God on the day you were married, and I'll do so by means of my own experience.

When we became engaged, Emilie was 17 years old and I was 22. She was beginning her senior year in high school, and I was starting my first year of teaching.

Since Emilie's family was Jewish and would not attend a Christian wedding in our church, we planned a very modest ceremony at the home of a family friend.

As we prepared for our wedding, Emilie and I were very much aware that the heart of the ceremony was to be the covenant we would enter into. We would be pledging to love one another at his or her most unlovely and unlovable moments. We would be promising to stand with one another no matter what came our way along life's path.

Now it's one thing to whisper such a pledge in private, but this pledge to each other—this sacred vow—was to be made in the presence of family and friends. Before I took that important step, I wrestled with very typical questions—"Is this the right choice? Will this marriage last for life? Will I be able to earn enough money to support a family? Am I really ready to give up being single? Emilie is so young—are we ready to be married?" Afterward, Emilie and I felt both reassured and strengthened to have received a voluntary and unconditional public commitment from one another. The wedding ceremony was a very special way of saying to each other, "I love you!"

And I can remember that ceremony as if it happened yesterday. Pastor Robert Hubbard had us repeat the following vows:

> In the name of God, I, Bob, take you, Emilie, to be my wife; to have and to hold from this day forward; for better, for worse; for richer, for poorer; in sickness and in health; to love, honor, and cherish, until we are parted by death. This is my solemn vow.
>
> In the name of God, I, Emilie, take you, Bob, to be my husband; to have and to hold from this day forward; for better, for worse; for

richer, for poorer; in sickness and in health; to love, honor, obey, and cherish, until we are parted by death. This is my solemn vow.

Again, those vows were made publicly and solemnly. Those vows were made "in the name of God." And those vows have strengthened our love for one another for 37 years.

Couples who elope or marry in secret miss out on the dimension of community witness and celebration which can so encourage and support two newlyweds. The public pronouncement of our vows before our family and friends reminded me that our marriage involved something bigger than two people who loved each other. I realized that, besides bringing together many other people than just the two of us, our wedding had a sacred and eternal significance. When we made our vows before God, we said to each other and to all the witnesses that God is the source of our love and that the purpose of our life together is to do His will and serve Him.

As Emilie and I repeated our vows to each other, the pastor made this pronouncement: "Those whom God has joined together, let no man put asunder. For as much as you, Bob and Emilie, have consented together in this sacred covenant and have declared the same before God and this company of friends, I pronounce you husband and wife. In the name of the Father and of the Son and of the Holy Spirit. Amen."

I had vowed before God, before Emilie, and before many witnesses to love and cherish my new wife. Through the years, I have come back again and again to those words of commitment that I spoke at 6:45 P.M. on Friday, September 30, 1955. They have served as a powerful reminder of the commitment to God which is the foundation of our marriage.

As the years have flown by, I have been very glad that God blessed our lives with those vows. They have been a signpost of the significance of marriage before God and kept us together when feelings of love have waned and the challenges of life have overwhelmed.

I share at length my own experience in hopes of encouraging you to reflect on your vows and to stand by that commitment you made to your husband today and when the going gets rough. May God graciously remind you of the solemn pledge you made on your wedding day and of the fact that you made that vow not only to your husband, but to God.

Marriage Vows for Today

Now imagine for a moment that your wedding is taking place today. If you were to rewrite the vows you spoke however many years ago, what would you promise to do? What commitments would you make? Thinking through your commitment to your husband in a fresh, new way like this can do much to revitalize your commitment to him. Consider the following samples of what other couples have written:

- "My commitment to you is to listen to your concerns each day for the purpose of having the kind of marriage we both want."

- "I realize that our love will change. I will work to maintain a high level of romance, courtship, and love in our relationship."

- "I pledge myself to confront problems when they arise and not retreat like a turtle into my shell."

- "I commit myself to you in times of joy and in times of problems. We will tackle and share our problems together."

- "I promise that I will never be too busy to look at the flowers with you."

- "I will respect your beliefs and capabilities which are different from mine and will not attempt to make you into a revised edition of me."

- "I will be open and honest with no secrets, and I desire you to be the same with me."

- "I will reflect the Word of God in my relationship with you."[3]

Now take several minutes to write out some vows for your marriage. This is a wonderful exercise for your husband to do, too. When the time is right—perhaps on a wedding anniversary or during a quiet weekend alone—share your rewritten and updated vows with one another. Discuss them and recommit your marriage to God. You'll find that these vows—written by two people who now have a real-life understanding of marriage as opposed to the two young innocents who originally spoke words of commitment to one another—can give renewed meaning and purpose to your marriage.

After the Wedding...

Several years ago, our friends Fred and Florence Littauer wrote the bestselling book *After Every Wedding Comes a Marriage*, and that title reflects a truth which engaged couples can't fully appreciate. That truth—that distinction between being in a wedding as a bride or groom and being in a marriage as a husband or wife—was in our minds as Emilie and I watched our two children make plans for their large church weddings. We knew that the wedding ceremony was only the beginning and that the real challenges come with marriage. We also knew all too well that a beautiful wedding is no indication that the marriage which follows will be beautiful.

And perhaps you were caught by surprise as you began to realize how difficult marriage can be. After all, none of us can ever really know what it means to be married until we are married. Consequently, we can find that return from the honeymoon a rather rude awakening to the very real challenges of two people becoming one and learning to live together. Those day-to-day challenges can indeed test the words of commitment we spoke to each other on that special day of music and lace and love.

Furthermore, we live in an age where commitment doesn't mean what it did a few decades ago. All around us and in a variety of contexts—in sports, business, politics, and even the family—we see people break their promises and walk away from their commitments. A person's word is no longer binding the way it once was.

Our commitments are also weakened by the world's message that we can "have it all." This lie from Satan encourages people to look for something better rather than try to improve what they have. Broken marriages, broken families, and broken people result when we walk away from the vows we made to one another and before God on our wedding day.

This lie, with its implication that we can and should be happy, also sows seeds of dissatisfaction with life. As I look around today, I see individuals and couples who are not content with their life. The apostle Paul, however, learned to be content whatever his circumstances— and his circumstances were sometimes very difficult (Philippians 4:11). Paul knew beatings, stonings, imprisonment, shipwreck, hunger, sleeplessness, cold, and danger from rivers, robbers, and false brethren (2 Corinthians 11:23-27). Paul's commitment to the Lord kept him strong despite the hardships, and your commitment to the Lord—spoken in your wedding vows—can keep you strong in your marriage.

Paul knew God to be the source of real staying power and true contentment, and we must turn to God, too, as we face the unfairness, evil, and hardship of the world. We can be content in Christ despite the hunger, wars, killings, disease, earthquakes, tornadoes, hurricanes, floods, fires, robberies, and social and civil injustices of our fallen world. Closer to home, we can be content in Christ despite the challenges, demands, and even empty times of marriage. That's what reviewing your wedding vows will tell you. Paul proclaimed, "I can do all things through Him who strengthens me" (Philippians 4:13), and you can claim that promise from God for yourself in your marriage. The God before whom you vowed to love your husband will enable you to stand by him.

Marriage and the Gospel

Susannah Wesley, the wife of the eighteenth-century evangelist John Wesley, once observed, "There are two things to do about the gospel—believe it and behave it." The easier part is to believe it; the harder part is to behave it. And that may be true of your wedding vows: the easier part is to believe the promises you made; the harder part is to act on those vows. As we live each day, however, we show the world how much we believe the gospel *and* our marriage vows by the way we behave. Marriage—with its stresses, trials, and inescapable closeness to another person—is certainly a test to see how we live out the gospel. In our marriage, for instance, we have every opportunity to share the fruit of the Spirit with our spouse (Galatians

5:22,23). All that God asks us to do and be as His son or daughter can be—and should be—worked out within a marriage relationship. Christian stewardship is also an issue in the arena of marriage: God will ask whether Emilie is a better Christian for having been married to me. Believing the gospel is one thing; living it is something very different—and our spouse will know better than anyone whether we are walking in God's path.

Far more than being merely an arena for living out the gospel, marriage can indeed be a wonderful blessing. Consider George Eliot's perspective on the union: "What greater thing is there for two human souls than to feel that they are joined for life—to strengthen each other in all labor, to rest in each other in all sorrow, to minister to each other in all pain, to be one with each other in silent unspeakable memories at the moment of the last parting."[4] May God help you believe these words anew and may He richly bless you as you live them out.

5

Stand by Your Femininity

Don't be concerned about the outward beauty that depends on jewelry, or beautiful clothes, or hair arrangement. Be beautiful inside, in your hearts, with the lasting charm of a gentle and quiet spirit which is so precious to God.

1 Peter 3:3,4 TLB

As a man, let me assure you that we men love to be in the presence of a real lady. Such a woman makes us men feel more masculine, more self-confident, and more relaxed (we don't worry about any hidden agenda). And a real lady affects us not because of how she looks or dresses, but because of who she is.

What do I mean by "real lady"? A woman who

worked in our local bank for years comes to mind. As she dealt with her customers, she somehow radiated peace. She always offered us tranquillity, warmth, friendliness, courtesy, and a welcoming spirit. In a woman, these traits can be very feminine, and we men respond favorably. The apostle Peter offered this perspective on femininity: "Let not your adornment be merely external . . . but let it be the hidden person of the heart, with the imperishable quality of a gentle and quiet spirit, which is precious in the sight of God" (1 Peter 3:3,4).

How do I define "feminine"? Not by a particular style, form, dress, or interior decorating. "Feminine" can take on an infinite variety of physical appearances. Instead, I see "feminine" as a softness, gentleness, and graciousness—and that's not to say that a woman cannot be the president of a corporation or a tough and aggressive participant in the business world. Underneath, though, a feminine woman will have a softness and graciousness that men simply don't have. To me, "feminine" also means that a woman has a sense of who she is apart from what she does; nurtures a strong spirituality; and manifests the fruit of the Spirit in every aspect of her life (Galatians 5:22,23). "Femininity" also brings to my mind a deep concern for her husband and children, the ability to submit to one's husband when appropriate (Ephesians 5:21), and the maternal awareness that she is raising not only her children but generations to come. Finally, a truly feminine woman understands the mystique of being a godly wife and mother.

The "gentle and quiet spirit" which Peter refers to, this tranquillity, this sense that a woman is at peace with herself, this ability to share the fruit of the Spirit with people she comes in contact with—these qualities result from a woman's relationship with God. When a woman has this inner peace, she doesn't feel any need to prove herself to her husband or anyone else. Confident in herself and aware of her God-given strengths, she doesn't feel compelled to use those strengths to control other people. She enjoys an inner contentment that isn't based on accomplishments, status, authority, power, or other people's opinions.

As I mentioned earlier, this woman of God has also learned the value of being versus doing. Too many women today have forgotten how to simply *be*. They have bought into the lie of doing and become highly obsessive-compulsive about getting work done. Like men, many women today are now more oriented toward doing, not being. As a result, they are cut off from their feminine feelings and nature.

A woman who walks closely with her God, however, is free from aggressiveness, competitiveness, and the need to prove her worth. Again, she may be aggressive and high-energy by temperament or competitive and very capable in the business world, but the fact is that she is affirmed not by other people but by her God. Such a woman "opens her mouth in wisdom, and the teaching of kindness is on her tongue" (Proverbs 31:26), and her family is blessed: "The heart of her husband trusts in her, and he will have no lack of gain. She does him good and not evil all the days of her life. . . . Her children rise up and bless her" (Proverbs 31:11,12,28). Such a woman doesn't try to attain greatness for herself, but she is an inspiration to the man of her life to rise to his own greatness and she supports him unconditionally in his search for fulfillment and achievement. And such a woman—one closely in tune with God—is indeed worthy of praise as she models godly values and high moral standards and truly reflects the feminine virtues of patience, silence, and faith. A woman's gentle and quiet spirit makes her a blessing to the people around her.

Gentleness, patience, and devotion to God—traits which I view as components of godly femininity—are qualities which hold society together and provide hope for the future, and, for whatever reason, those qualities seem to be more feminine than masculine. You may not like the responsibility that's placed upon you, but history shows that as the woman goes, so goes the family. You give meaning and purpose to a home. You are the heartbeat of the home, pumping vital blood into the family system by setting the spirit and tone of the home. Without your softer, more feminine qualities, we men would become aggressive animals with hungered appetites for the exotic and the erotic. You help us and our children establish and live by moral standards.

The Mystique of Femininity

The femininity I have described teaches, inspires, and civilizes. It brings glory to God and hope to His world. And, on a less tangible or practical level, such femininity also has a real mystique about it, but many women don't capitalize on this mystique. Their grandmothers—who were students of men and knew what made men tick *and* what made them ticked!—knew how their femininity affected men. Today, however, so many young women (even Christian women, unfortunately) waste their feminine attributes, abilities, and gifts. They move in with their boyfriends, cook for them, clean for them, sleep with them—and then wonder why their young man doesn't want to commit to marriage. Again, the grandmothers understood that having a home, hot meals, and clean clothes mean a lot to a man, so they didn't cash in these feminine offerings—they didn't move in with a man—until after marriage.

One mother wise about the feminine mystique offered this advice to her future daughter-in-law. Her son was a minister and an avid reader who spent large amounts of time in the library studying and preparing for the next Sunday's sermon. The mother said this to the soon-to-be bride: "John loves to study and often works late into the night at the library. Don't try to change him, but always have his dinner in a warm oven and keep a pot of coffee on the stove." The young lady listened to her future mother-in-law and, at last account, she had been married to Pastor John for over 40 years.

Pastor John's wife truly understood the magic of being a woman. As the Living Bible puts it, she was an example of "that kind of deep beauty ... seen in the saintly women of old who trusted God and fitted in with her husband's plans" (1 Peter 3:5 TLB). This type of woman can be irresistible to men. Even twentieth-century women acknowledge the mystique. Consider what Dr. Toni Grant wrote in *Being a Woman*: "It is women to whom men look to bring out their gentler natures and their highest ideals, inflame their passions, and motivate them to achievement. This feminine woman is a rarity in today's culture, and the traditional male still seeks valiantly for her inspiration."[1] Even today, the mystique can work. Are you letting it work for you to enrich your marriage?

The Call to Submission

Perhaps the idea of using the magic of being feminine sounds quite old-fashioned. To introduce yet another "old-fashioned" idea (and this one is strictly biblical), let me ask you a few questions. Are you tired of being a leader? Do you find yourself often feeling as if you are forcing your ideas on others, being overly assertive, and always choosing how to discipline the children and where to go on vacation? Are you wanting to become more feminine—to nurture a gentle and quiet spirit and a deeper devotion to the Lord? Are you wondering how to gain or regain that feminine mystique which can enrich your marriage? I think the best way for a woman to become more feminine is to become less masculine. This sounds dated and certainly out of step with the times, but it is based on guidelines given by our wise and loving God.

In the Bible, we see that God created both men and women in His image. One is not the superior to the other; they are equal and complementary. Our different functions within marriage have nothing to do with superiority or inferiority. Instead, equality in our Creator God's eyes calls both husbands and wives to mutual respect and affirmation based in the awareness that we and our spouse are created in God's image and, as fellow believers, are called to "be subject to one another in the fear of Christ" (Ephesians 5:21).

In Ephesians 5:22,23, a well-known but often misunderstood passage on marriage, we find God's instructions on leadership in the home. The passage reads: "You wives must submit to your husbands' leadership in the same way you submit to the Lord" (TLB). Before reacting too strongly, remember that this is not a plan developed by a human being. It was given to us by God. Why? Because it really works! When wives submit to their husbands in the same way they submit to the Lord, a marriage can be spared of power plays, conflicts, and indecision.

Many women today have a difficult time with the word *submission*, but I define it simply as "arranging oneself under the authority of another." If your husband asks you to do something contrary to a moral or biblical principle, I don't believe you must submit to his leadership. But I do believe that biblical submission calls for a wife to trust, respect, and honor her husband. When women instead harbor resentment, resistance, or rebellion, love can't grow. Furthermore, Toni Grant asserts that "women are best able to live out their feminine aspects when they give over some of their male dominance to the opposite sex freely and unconditionally. When a woman is willing to do this, she inspires enormous confidence in her man and enhances not only his masculinity, but her own femininity as well."[2]

Becoming More Feminine

There are other ways you can enhance your femininity as well, and many of those ways will be unique to you. Take a pencil and jot down activities that help you feel feminine:

_____	_____
_____	_____
_____	_____
_____	_____

Are you doing any of these activities regularly? Put an "X" next to those. Now look at those activities which you haven't made time for. Choose at least one to do this week and then another next week. Begin to incorporate these into your everyday life.

As you made your list, did you consider the possibilities listed below? These activities can put you more in touch with your feminine side:

- Buy some fresh flowers for your home. (Silk flowers will do, too!)

- Light a candle or small oil lamp by the kitchen sink, the nightstand, or the bathtub.
- Get a new haircut or add something new to your makeup collection.
- Read a love story or poem.
- Buy that lacy dress you've been looking at for the last month.
- Pamper yourself with a new bottle of perfume.
- Buy a new set of sheets—the kind with soft ruffles on the edges.
- Start a daily exercise program. (If you don't have access to a gym or videotape aerobics lessons, walk!)
- Unclutter your bedroom. Reserve it for sleep and romance.
- Linger in a bathtub spiced with fragrant oils.
- Take time to enjoy a cup of tea or coffee (decaffeinated of course!).
- Find some colorful stationery, use ink that isn't blue or black, add a sticker or a rubber stamp that represents something about you.
- Develop your own trademark (ducks, chickens, a certain color, flowers, teddy bears, etc.).
- Read the Old Testament's Song of Solomon.
- Buy some new lingerie for tonight—or that next weekend getaway!
- Give a special gift—something extravagant—to a special woman friend.
- Call your husband at work and tell him you love him.
- Spend quality time with each one of your children.
- Bake a batch of chocolate chip cookies.
- Cook a favorite family meal—or the favorite of one family member—and set a special table.

- Spray your home with a fresh fragrance of pot-pourri.
- Call a friend.
- Write a note to someone you have not written to for a while.
- Greet your husband at the door with a kiss. Smell nice and look good, too.
- Meet a new friend.
- Attend a Bible study.
- Buy a copy of *Victoria* magazine.

Don't try to do all these different activities at the same time! This is not another "Have to Do" list. Instead, let these suggestions help you become aware of opportunities you have to discover and enjoy your feminine side.

A Feminine Serenity

And those opportunities listed above contrast sharply with the pace and noise of the world we live in. Teenagers blast their stereos, television often adds a constant background noise to our homes, and freeways are deafening even a mile away. What happened to quietness? Where did serenity go?

My dictionary defines "serene" as "calm, clear, unruffled, peaceful, placid, tranquil, [and] unperturbed." Do those words describe anyplace or anyone you know? Maybe the Grand Canyon. And maybe a wise woman who has discovered the peace of our Lord and learned how to rest in Him. That dictionary definition of "serene" describes so few places and people in our world which says that we have to do more and more and more, faster and faster and faster. We have fast-food restaurants, drive-through lines, car phones, second-day mail, next-day mail, and facsimile machines—at home and even in the car!

Do you ever want to, with me, scream, "Help! Get me off of this merry-go-round! I can't take it anymore!" I yearn for peace and quiet, but where do I turn? You and I must turn to God. We have to become quiet inside. Chuck Swindoll comments about the quietness we need today:

> You know something? That still, small voice will never shout. God's methods don't change because we are so noisy and busy. He is longing for your attention, your undivided and full attention. He wants to talk with you in times of quietness (with the TV off) about your need for understanding, love, compassion, patience, self-control, a calm spirit, genuine humility . . . and wisdom. But He won't run to catch up. He will wait and wait until you finally sit in silence and listen.[3]

We need to be quiet before the Lord, to experience His peace and His restoring touch. We need to listen to what He would teach us and hear where He would have us go. You will benefit greatly from such times with your heavenly Father.

Let me also say that a man responds well to a woman who is serene. She settles the environment just by her presence. The serene woman will be at peace with those around her. She will be sensitive to nature, aware of all aspects of her womanhood, and willing to help make the world better. Furthermore, she is not so rushed that she can't give you her time. Her home will reflect this serenity, welcoming people to relax. Guests will ask, "How do you ever leave this home? It's so comfortable! I feel such tranquillity when I'm with you, and it's so good to relax." Has anyone told you those things lately? Why not?

Again, Toni Grant offers a modern woman's

perspective on serenity: "A woman without serenity seems hardly a woman at all; she is nervous, high-strung, all 'bent out of shape' and utterly impatient."[4] One key to finding that serenity is learning to let life happen around you. You really don't have to be involved in everything. Sometimes it is very right for you to say no. You also need to let go of those things you can't control if you are to experience serenity. Again, serenity and tranquillity are gifts of God. They come when we trust Him as our Lord, Shepherd, Guide, and Protector.

A Lesson from the Past

Let me suggest another reason many women fail to experience a sense of tranquillity or peace by asking a few questions. Do you like yourself? Are you fulfilled? Do you have purpose? Positive answers to these questions cost. Fulfillment and the peace it offers don't come free. You will work and sacrifice as you live out your purpose and find fulfillment as a woman of God, a wife, and a mother.

Consider Sarah Edwards, the wife of theologian and preacher Jonathan Edwards and the mother of 11 children. According to one biographer, Sarah's children and her children's children, through the generations, were a tribute to this woman in their distinguished positions as college presidents, professors, attorneys, judges, physicians, senators, governors, and even a vice president of the United States. What influenced 1400 of Sarah Edwards' descendants to become such fine citizens? One author suggests that, being a deeply Christian woman, Sarah treated her children with patience, courtesy, respect, and love. She taught her children to work and deal with what life brought their way. Convinced that until children can obey their parents they will never be obedient to God, Sarah was also a firm disciplinarian, but one who never resorted to words of anger. Her home emanated love and harmony. And what were the results of her efforts as homemaker and mother?

As [biographer] Elizabeth Dodds makes abundantly clear in her book, a mother is not merely rearing her one generation of children. She is also affecting future generations for good or ill. All the love, nurture, education, and character-building that spring from Mother's work influence those sons and daughters. The results show up in the children's accomplishments, attitudes toward life and parenting capacity. For example, one of Sarah Edwards' grandsons, Timothy Dwight, president of Yale (echoing Lincoln) said, "All that I am and all that I shall be, I owe to my mother."[5]

What can women of the twentieth century learn from Sarah Edwards, wife, mother, and homemaker? Consider the following possibilities:

As one ponders this praise [by Timothy Dwight], the question arises: Are we women unhappy in our mothering and wife role because we make too little, rather than too much of that role? Do we see what we have to give our husbands and children as minor rather than major, and consequently send them into the world without a healthy core identity and strong spiritual values?

It was the great investment of time that mothers like Sarah Edwards made in the lives of their children that garnered each such high praise. One can't teach a child to read in an hour or stretch a child's mind in a few days.[6]

Sarah spent many untiring hours serving her husband and children. A colonial homemaker, Sarah had candles and clothes to make, food to prepare from scratch, the fire to keep burning, and the garden to tend. Her responsibilities were many and the demands on her great, yet she seemed to offer her family a sense of serenity as she cared for them. Can a modern woman do the same?

Becoming Serene

Despite how different our world is from colonial America, I believe a wife and mother can indeed make her home a place of serenity. It starts when she herself discovers and nurtures a serenity that God alone gives. Here are some ways to develop a serenity that will weather the demands of being a wife and mother.

- Sit in a quiet room for 5, 10, or 15 minutes and reflect on what God is doing in your life.
- Wait upon the Lord. Listen for Him to direct, encourage, guide, and teach.
- Just sit and hold hands with your husband and think about God's love, power, and peace.
- Turn on some peaceful music. Pass on the loud sounds and high volume.
- Take a walk—at the beach, on a mountain trail, in a snowy meadow. Ski down a hill or watch the leaves fall off the trees.
- Take a warm bubble bath.
- Draw a picture.
- Find a new hobby.
- Eliminate some of the confusion in your life.
- Don't drive over the speed limit.
- Ride a bicycle instead of driving a car.
- Feed the ducks in the park.
- Tell your husband that you love him.

- Say no to someone who wants you to do something that you don't want to do.
- Don't volunteer for anything new for two weeks.
- Speak quietly and smile when you talk.
- Try writing out your prayers for a week.
- Start keeping a journal of your daily events and feelings.

Again, this is not another list of "Have to Do" items. But I challenge and encourage you to choose an activity to do. See if you don't discover a new sense of serenity—and be aware of how that affects your husband, your children, and your home.

In *All I Really Need to Know I Learned in Kindergarten*, Robert Fulghum suggests that your new serenity and quiet spirit is very much needed in our noisy world. He tells of villagers in the Solomon Islands who fell a tree by screaming at it for 30 days. The tree does die, confirming their theory that hollering kills its spirit. Fulghum then considers the things that he and his neighbors yell at: the wife, the kids, the telephone, the lawn mower that won't start, traffic, umpires, machines. Then he offers this observation:

> Don't know what good it does. Machines and things just sit there. Even kicking doesn't always help. As for people, well, the Solomon Islanders may have a point. Yelling at living things does tend to kill the spirit in them. Sticks and stones may break our bones, but words will break our hearts.[7]

Oh, if we could only remember this each time we want to overpower someone with a loud voice. How much better a quiet and gentle spirit! How much better the feminine gifts of tranquillity and serenity!

6

Stand by Your Man's Needs

Then the Lord God said,
"It is not good for the man to be alone;
I will make him a helper suitable for him."

Genesis 2:18

B ob, would you mind helping me move this table? I'm not strong enough!" I love to hear Emilie say that she needs me. Her need allows me to be what God created me to be: the stronger partner, the protector, the provider. If I'm not allowed to help my wife, one of my purposes as a husband and a man is taken away from me.

And examples of men helping people in need are everywhere, especially in emergency situations. In March 1992, Southern California had about seven days of torrential rain, at one point receiving six inches in a six-hour period. Rushing waters washed over cars, and 40 people had to be helicoptered to safety. Teenagers were swept away when normally dry riverbeds became swollen and powerful rivers. Mud slides destroyed homes and lives. And in all these situations men risked their lives trying to help people in need. The media reported numerous tales about how men offered their assistance despite the danger. When there is a need, men respond! Just like a truck driver who stops alongside the freeway to assist a stranded motorist, a man who recognizes a need or hears it expressed will respond. We simply have to know we're needed.

But Who Needs Help?

In our culture, however, we consider ourselves very capable. We pride ourselves on our self-sufficiency and ability to get things done. We don't need help from anyone! And that is as true for women as it is for men.

Many women today are hard-charging, assertive, and very competent. The wise woman of the nineties, however, is beginning to slow down. She has realized that enough's enough and is giving up her attempt to be Superwoman and/or Supermom. She has realized that the elusive goal isn't worth what it's costing her to try to reach it. Such a woman, free of society's unrealistic expectations and its call to be independent, can say, "Honey, I need you. Would you please help me?"

Show Him You Need Him

One way to melt a man is to show him that you truly need him. He needs to be needed. The simple, direct statement "I need your help" reinforces your husband's masculinity. Most husbands would not refuse a wife's straightforward expression of a need:

- "Will you please help me with this lamp?"
- "Would you hold me while I cry? It's so hard to see my mother suffering...."
- "Please help me figure out what the instructor wants here."
- "Could we go to the beach this weekend—just the two of us?"

Whether your request is large or small, ask your husband for help. Let him know that you need him. And, the way life goes, you won't have to make up needs. We all have plenty of very real needs that can be expressed. We—men and women alike—simply have to learn to express them.

In her book *Being a Woman*, clinical psychologist Toni Grant offers you wives this advice:

> It is important that a man feels that he fulfills a purpose in your life, that he somehow makes the woman feel better, safer, and more beautiful than she was before. He needs to know that his masculine presence makes a difference to her feminine well being; otherwise two people may have met person to person, but not man to woman.[1]

Scripture also teaches the importance of having someone there to help us when we are in need. The writer of Ecclesiastes notes that "two are better than one because they have a good return for their labor. For if either of them falls, the one will lift up his companion. But woe to the one who falls when there is not another to lift him up" (4:9,10). In Galatians, Paul calls believers to "bear one another's burdens, and thus fulfill the law of Christ" (6:2). Again and again, Scripture reminds us of the importance of having someone come alongside to help when times are difficult. Reaching out when we're in need helps that need be met and also creates a special bond with the person we let come near.

I encourage you to let your husband come near, whether your need is large or small, emotional, physical, spiritual, intellectual, or material. One of his key roles is to provide for and protect his family. When you allow your husband to provide for your needs, you bring out his masculine side. You'll probably also find yourself feeling closer to him who has just taken care of you in some way.

Knowing and Meeting Your Mate's Needs

Needing to be needed is only one of a man's basic needs, but a woman is often unaware of this need or any of her husband's other needs. Likewise, we husbands are not always aware of what our wives need! Why are we so blind to each other's needs? Perhaps many of us are looking for what we can get rather than what we can give in our marriage. Others of us are more than willing and ready to give, but we just don't know what to give or how we can best meet our mate's needs. In fact, after 37 years of marriage, Emilie and I are still trying to figure this one out!

In *His Needs, Her Needs*, author Willard F. Harley, Jr. lists five basic needs husbands and wives bring to a marriage:

Men's Needs

1. Sexual Fulfillment
2. Recreational Companionship
3. An Attractive Spouse
4. Domestic Support
5. Admiration

Women's Needs

1. Affection
2. Conversation
3. Honesty and Openness
4. Financial Support
5. Family Commitment[2]

Recognizing and meeting these needs for one another will mean a stronger marriage and the ability to get through the rocky times that come. A wife benefits greatly when her husband recognizes her needs and does his best to meet them—without always having to be asked! In keeping with the purpose of this book, though, I will focus on a husband's needs and how you can meet them.

1. Sexual Fulfillment

At a men's conference, the speaker was addressing the topic "Sexuality in Marriage." Taking a survey of his audience, he asked the 80 men, "How many of you have sex three times a week?" A few of the young married men raised their hands. "How many of you have sex once a week?" A few of the 40-year-olds raised their hands. The speaker finally worked his way to "How many of you have sex once a year?" At that question, an elderly man in the back row jumped up, waving his hand vigorously. Puzzled by this man's enthusiasm about having sex only once a year, the speaker said, "Why are you so excited about having sex once a year?" The elderly man replied, "Tonight's the night!"

When "tonight's the night," sex truly is something to get excited about, but often husbands and wives don't share the same level of excitement. The key to mutual sexual fulfillment is intimacy, and sexual intimacy is directly linked to other types of intimacy. Are you married to a workaholic? Does your husband spend so many hours earning a living that he spends little, if any, time with you? When, as a result, you are lonely, unfulfilled, or even angry, it's hard to respond positively to your husband's sexual advances. The title of Dr. Kevin Leman's book—*Sex Begins in the Kitchen*—makes an important point that many husbands need to hear. We men shouldn't wait until bedtime to start getting romantic. We need to set the stage at breakfast with kind words and loving touches. We need to leave a thoughtful note where our wife will find it, give her a call during the day, and return home from work with a hug, a kiss, a wink, and a listening ear. Our wives need more than our sexual prowess—they need us!

Once the lights are out, we men need to slow down. We need to tell our wife that we love her and take time for plenty of foreplay—for gentle caresses, loving hugs, and sweet words. After intercourse, we need to take some time for more talking and tenderness as we assure her further of our love for her. Developing intimacy like this—and you women know this all too well—will enable a wife to better meet her husband's need for sexual fulfillment and allow her to experience that fulfillment herself.

Let me add, though, women, that it's okay for you to initiate sexual intimacy. God gave women as well as men the desire for sex, so it makes sense that at times you will initiate the intimacy. In fact, Emilie has planned some of our most exciting and romantic evenings. Sometimes, for instance, she prepares a "love basket." She takes a large basket lined with a lacy tablecloth and fills it with favorite foods, sparkling cider, a candle, and even a bunch of fresh flowers. The setting for the meal can be in the park, at the beach, at an outdoor concert, or in the bedroom with candlelight and soft music. (There is a complete chapter on the love basket in Emilie's book *More Hours in My Day*.) Romance like this promotes an atmosphere of love and leads to mutual fulfillment, sexual and otherwise, and there are many ways to add romance to your marriage. Send flowers or make a phone call to say, "I love you." Leave a sexy note for your mate or send a card that expresses your love. Give your mate physical attention. Hold hands, touch tenderly, and hug and kiss often. (Be patient if your mate comes from a home which was not as openly affectionate as yours.) Romance leads to emotional intimacy, a key contributor to sexual intimacy.

Another key to sexual fulfillment has to do with the sexual act itself. Having achieved emotional intimacy, many Christian couples wonder what kind of sexual intimacy is appropriate for believers. Again and again Emilie and I are asked, "Is it okay for Christian couples to...?" In response, we usually refer to Hebrews 13:4—"Let marriage be held in honor among all, and let the marriage bed be undefiled"—as the guideline that we use to determine what kind of lovemaking is appropriate. Emilie and I talk to each other to see if the activity in question would enrich our intimacy. If we both feel that the activity would bring us closer together and if both of us would enjoy that activity, we go ahead with it.

Sometimes a couple puts a certain lovemaking technique on hold because one partner is uncomfortable with the idea, and that is as it should be. We must be very sensitive to our partner's desires and not pressure him or her into doing something uncomfortable. After all, our sexuality is a gift that is to promote intimacy! If you aren't sure about certain practices, apply the principle of Proverbs 3:6—"In all thy ways acknowledge him, and he shall direct thy paths" (KJV). Talk to the Lord together about the proposed activity. It's amazing how God will reveal the proper answer for you.

Husbands and wives experience sexual fulfillment when emotional intimacy has already been achieved, when we agree on appropriate activities, and—the third key—when we are students of our mates and therefore able to meet their needs. What better way to learn what our mate needs and enjoys than to ask questions and discuss feelings, needs, and expectations? Emilie doesn't hesitate to ask me if there is anything I would like her to do for me sexually that we aren't doing or anything that I don't want her to do—and I freely ask her the same questions. Such frank discussions can eliminate assumptions and pave the way for deeper intimacy and greater fulfillment in sex. When Emilie tells me where she likes to be touched and stroked, I can more completely meet her needs and enrich our lovemaking.

Let me add a few more thoughts on sexual intimacy. I would encourage husbands and wives to alternate the roles of giver and receiver in foreplay and intercourse. Don't get into a rut. Keep some mystery in your sex life. The sex act alone—without romantic moments, open communication, and mutual contentment in the relationship—can become shallow and lonely. Also, through verbal and nonverbal communication, we need to express our wants and preferences to our mate and encourage our mate to do the same. Sex in such a context of openness, trust, acceptance, and love is indeed rich and fulfilling for both partners.

God's Idea of Intimacy

The Bible's teaching on marriage has helped Emilie and me learn about God's master plan for husbands and wives. One of the most important passages we have discovered is 1 Corinthians 7:1-5:

> It is good for a man not to touch a woman. But because of immoralities, let each man have his own wife, and let each woman have her own husband. Let the husband fulfill his duty

to his wife, and likewise also the wife to her husband. The wife does not have authority over her own body, but the husband does; and likewise also the husband does not have authority over his own body, but his wife does. Stop depriving one another, except by agreement for a time that you may devote yourselves to prayer, and come together again lest Satan tempt you because of your lack of self-control.

These verses provide four solid guidelines for couples who desire love and intimacy in their relationship.

First, be faithful to one person. Sexual immorality was rampant in the city of Corinth, the home of the church to which Paul is writing here—and our society is, sadly, quite similar to that ancient world. Christian men and women today, for instance, live in a world that accepts extramarital affairs and divorce. Places of employment and the local gym are often scenes of temptation. God's Word, however, clearly commands us to be faithful to our spouse (Exodus 20:14; Matthew 5:27-32; 19:18).

Second, be available to each other. A husband is to give of himself to fulfill his wife's needs, and a wife is to give of herself to fulfill her husband's needs. We are to freely ask for and give affection to one another. Don't be afraid to tell your mate that you are in the mood for love and always be ready to respond when your partner is in the mood. If you are too tired to enjoy each other and meet each other's needs, you may need to eliminate other commitments and activities in order to, in compliance with this scriptural directive, be the kind of spouse God calls you to be.

Third, submit to each other. Closely related to being available to our partners is being willing to submit to their sexual desires and needs. Wives, if your mate wants to make love, you should not withhold yourself from him, but submit to his desires. Be open about your desires and your energy level to arrive at a mutually satisfying plan for the evening. Be aware, too, that your willingness to meet your partner's sexual needs and desires—besides being an act of obedience to Scripture—may very well prevent him from falling into moral sin with someone who seems more ready to meet his needs than you are.

Finally, keep on meeting your spouse's sexual needs. Paul notes that the only exception to this guideline is taking time for prayer and fasting. Other than at these specified times, a husband and wife should be available to each other and always seeking to meet the other's needs.

The Bible offers rich insight into the marriage relationship. Consider, for instance, that the New Testament writers liken Jesus' relationship to the church to the relationship between a husband and wife. I encourage you to spend some time studying what God's Word teaches about your marriage. Knowing and following the Creator's master plan will enrich your marriage sexually and otherwise.

Intimate Tips for Women

When Emilie talks to women about how to build intimacy in their marriages, she often directs them to the teachings of 1 Peter 3:1-6. Whether or not your husband is a believer, Emilie says, he will respond favorably if you follow these scriptural guidelines:

- Be submissive to your husband. Don't resist him or rebel against him.
- Demonstrate your Christian faith through your lifestyle. Don't preach.
- Be loyal to your husband in every way.

- Take care to remain attractive on the outside.
- Develop a quiet and gentle spirit that is inwardly attractive.

I would add that a woman should never criticize or attack her husband. A man's outward display of strength—however irritating that display may be—is often a cover-up for feelings of insecurity. When a woman attacks her man's ego, she certainly doesn't foster the intimacy she desires in the relationship. Instead, her husband may become withdrawn and noncommunicative, angry, and resentful. He won't respond to his critical wife with sensitivity, understanding, and compassion, and he may find himself unable to perform sexually. Also, he may be easily tempted to infidelity by a woman who understands his needs and will build up rather than tear down his ego. So rather than attack your husband, respect him and encourage him. Your husband needs to know that he is important to you and your children. When he knows that you believe in him and support him, he will be much more open and ready to be intimate with you.

Is Intimacy Possible?

Are you wondering whether real intimacy is even possible in your marriage? I want to assure you that it is. Genuine intimacy comes, first, when both you and your husband are willing to submit yourselves to each other out of reverence for Christ (see Ephesians 5:21). For 37 years, such mutual submission has protected Emilie and me from Satan who would have based his attacks on a prideful unwillingness to bend, accommodate, and submit to one another.

Know, too, that intimacy doesn't just happen. It takes persistent prayer and discipline to apply God's principles—principles which encourage intimacy—to your marriage. Again I challenge you to study God's Word on your own and with your spouse to learn what He says about love, sex, and intimacy in married life.

I also challenge you to look at yourself as honestly as you can. What qualities would make you a better wife? Where is God calling you to welcome His transforming Spirit into your heart? Ask God to help you see where you can be more the wife He wants you to be. Then prayerfully set some goals for yourself and pursue them doggedly.

Finally, continue to love the Lord with all your heart. By actively loving God and walking closely with Him, you plug yourself into His infinite and divine love which will feed your love for your husband and foster intimacy in your marriage. Be a doer of the Word in your marriage. Let your obedience to God's commands to serve and to love one another (and His command includes your husband!) bring new life and new closeness to your marriage. After all, God created sex and marriage, and He desires that you find love and intimacy in His creation.

2. Recreational Companionship

We've spent a lot of time looking at the item that tops the list of what men need. Sexual fulfillment is indeed important to us men, but now let's move on to the next need we men have—recreational companionship. Think back to those early courting days. Do you have memories of tennis, golf, hiking, camping, sporting events, and Lakers' basketball? Now that you have been married a few years and have a child or two, have you stopped doing those things? Or maybe your husband still enjoys those activities, but you are happier reading books, listening to good music, watching a good romance movie on television, or spending an evening at the theater. Or maybe you're the athlete and your husband prefers more sedentary activities. Do you remember how you and your husband used to love doing everything together? Are you wondering what went wrong along the way? Or are you wondering if it's even important that you and your mate aren't sharing pastimes and fun?

In response to that last question, let me say that Willard Harley's experience points to recreational companionship as the most important male need after sex. To me, that finding underscores the importance of playing together. Think about those couples you know who seem to have a strong marriage. The couples I know like that certainly exhibit an ability to enjoy each other's interests. And enjoying each other's interests doesn't mean that she plays tennis only and always with him or that he won't go out on the golf course without her. It means that spouses are interested and supportive of each other's recreation.

Our son, Brad, for instance, married a woman who likes to run, swim, bicycle, exercise, and sweat just as he does. Maria participates in many of his recreational activities. In our case, however, Emilie is not very athletic, but she does encourage and support my interest in sports. Likewise, I spend time with her doing what she enjoys doing—things like going out to dinner to celebrate a special occasion, attending the theater, or sharing a book. Emilie and I work together to give each other the freedom to enjoy our personal interests *and* to enjoy what the other person likes. Such compromise and sharing of our time keeps us growing together, something that separate vacations and long-term or frequent solo outings would not allow. In fact, such separateness can be very dangerous to a marriage relationship—and it's not even what we men always want.

Although the media shows the boys out fishing, drinking beer, and saying, "It doesn't get better than this!" we men do want our wives to share fun and recreational activities with us. Certainly many men's activities may be riskier, sweatier, and dirtier than women enjoy, and women's activities may be too quiet or passive. Emilie's choice of a movie, for instance, reflects her preference for softness, romance, and tenderness. I don't receive the same response to an invitation to a Clint Eastwood movie that I do when I ask her to see a romance! Again, compromise is called for—as is balance—and recreational compromises might include lunch or dinner out, a picnic, a walk, shopping, and attending various cultural events.

At times, however, men need to be with men and women need to be with women. After all, we have different needs and we have different things to give to one another. I'm sure you know the satisfaction of "girl talk." No matter how good a listener your husband is, there is something qualitatively different about sharing the latest event with a special girlfriend. She gives you something that your husband can't give and so meets a need of yours that your husband can't meet. Likewise, some of my male friends give me things that Emilie can't and in doing so meet some of my needs that, through no fault of her own, Emilie can't meet. It's a fact of life that our mate is not going to meet all our needs, and that's why same-sex friendships are so important to a healthy marriage.

But again let me emphasize that balance is important. The time we spend with our spouse needs to take priority over the time we spend with our same-sex friends. Willard Harley says the following: "When you do things separately, you have a tendency to grow apart, each experiencing your most enjoyable moments of fun and relaxation without the other. Couples with separate recreational interests miss a golden opportunity. They often spend their most enjoyable moments in the company of someone else. It stands to reason that the person with whom you share the most enjoyable moments will give you the greatest dividends."[3]

What do these words say to you? Do they help you answer the questions raised earlier—"What went wrong along the way?" Maybe as you and your husband have made choices about how to use your time, you've dropped some activities which you could be sharing. We can't say yes to everything, but—in one of the Barnes' favorite mottoes—we need to "say no to good things and save our yeses for the best." And wouldn't it be more beneficial to your marriage to find some recreational activities you can share?

3. An Attractive Spouse

Men value sexual fulfillment, recreational companionship, and, third, an attractive spouse. And what is attractive? The Bible offers this answer: "Don't be concerned about the outward beauty that depends on jewelry, or beautiful clothes, or hair arrangement. Be beautiful inside, in your hearts, with the lasting charm of a gentle and quiet spirit which is so precious to God. That kind of deep beauty was seen in the saintly women of old, who trusted God and fitted in with their husbands' plans" (1 Peter 3:3-5 TLB).

Scripture calls women to be godly and to develop an inward beauty, but wise women today also work to make themselves pleasing to their husband's eye—and that's right on target. Now, as a woman, you might not feel that the externals are very important, but doesn't looking nice make you feel better about yourself? Furthermore, externals are important because we men are aroused sexually by visual stimulation. When Emilie looks good, I look at her often and I like what I see. When men aren't proud of what they see in their wife, they become more vulnerable to having an affair. A pleasing appearance will invite your husband to touch and hold you—and no one else. Besides, your husband wants to be proud of you whether at home or in public, and I saw that clearly when I was growing up.

When I was a young boy, my mother wore current fashions and popular colors even though we were a low middle-class family. (You don't have to have a lot of money to look attractive!) When Dad came home, she always looked fashionable. She never left home with curlers in her hair or a bandanna wrapped around her head—she didn't want to embarrass herself if she ran into friends. Today, Mom is 78 years old and still outwardly attractive. And, funny thing, I married a woman just like Mom. Emilie has always presented herself well. When we go out together, I'm proud to introduce her to my friends. (In fact, many companies today interview the wife right along with the husband when he applies for a top management job. The business community knows how great an asset a wife can be to her husband and, rightly or wrongly, bases that judgment greatly on appearance.)

Every married woman needs to ask herself, "Am I looking my best when I am with my husband? Is he proud of my personal appearance?" If you feel you could make yourself more appealing and attractive, know that the resources available are many, ranging from self-help books, friends who will give suggestions, color and wardrobe seminars, and department store consultants who will assist you in developing a new you. And you might follow the example of a friend of ours....

Our friend has a specific plan of action to get ready

for her husband's arrival home. Each day at 4:00 P.M., she takes a shower or bath, powders and perfumes, combs her hair, and dresses informally. She lives according to another Barnes motto: "A husband should be sad when he leaves for work in the morning, and a wife should be glad to see him come home in the evening." When her husband arrives, her appearance shows that she has been waiting for him and that she cares that he has returned. I encourage you to pay attention to how you look for your husband. You—and he and your marriage—will definitely benefit!

4. Domestic Support

What do men value besides sexual fulfillment, recreational companionship , and an attractive spouse? Next on the list is support on the home front. I know that from experience and I know that from the mail which Emilie receives, specifically letters from men whose wives make great improvements in their home-making and organizational skills after attending one of our seminars. What happens in three hours that changes a wife? The secret isn't a little pill or a magic word. Instead, Emilie offers a biblical perspective on being a wife and homemaker, holds out the hope that women can indeed change the way their home is functioning, and shares ideas about how to lighten the load and even make homemaking fun. That kind of message is important because, for one reason, men need to know that their wives can handle the household and children in an organized and efficient way. The stereotypical male fantasy of coming home to a well-cooked meal, cooperative and well-behaved children, and a kiss at the door is not too far off what we men really do want!

Why is an organized, smoothly functioning home important to a man? Because, for one reason, we need a place to unwind after a day at work. We can feel drained after solving the problems, dealing with the challenges, and feeling the stresses of the day. We need to not be needed right away! When I arrived home, I used to always say to Emilie, "You think I'm home, but I just sent my body ahead of me!" In reality, I wouldn't be home for another 30 minutes. During that half-hour, I regrouped. I didn't handle any emergencies or deal with any bad news. I'd often get a cold drink, sit in my favorite chair, and even take a brief nap. That time allowed me to change gears. After that 30 minutes, I was truly home and able to function as a member of the family. I appreciated Emilie giving me this time to adjust, and she was able to do so because the home was functioning smoothly.

But, you ask, what can be done when both spouses work outside the home? In that situation, the couple needs to come up with a division of labor so that both the wife and the husband have their needs met. This division of labor often happens rather easily when a couple is first married. Then there is a lot of give-and-take because the husband is accustomed to taking care of himself in some fashion, and he usually continues along fine until the children arrive. At that point, he may worry about not having enough money, take on another job, and begin to resent helping out at home. Tired from a full day, irritated by freeway traffic, and frustrated with his inappreciative boss, he comes home stressed out. If the wife also works out of the home, she has identical stresses and pressures on her. Such a situation can take a serious toll on a marriage relationship. But you already know that. You want answers!

A solution may come when a couple looks closely at how they are currently using their time and energy around the house. This exercise is easier when the household responsibilities are divided into four categories:[4]

1. **Income-generating activities**—Work that earns money for family living expenses falls into this category. (Does not include volunteer work.)

2. **Child Care**—All tasks dealing with feeding, dressing, supervising, and caring for your children.

3. **Household Responsibilities**—Includes cooking, cleaning, washing, ironing, shopping, and organizing the home.

4. **Repair and Maintenance of the Home, Automobile, and Mechanical Possessions**—Includes mowing the lawn, painting the house, repairing the car, and fixing broken toys.

Using these four categories, develop a work inventory list. What do you and your husband do in each area of responsibility? List your responsibilities.

Husband	**Wife**
Income Generating Activities	
1. Account executive	1. Salesclerk
2. Financial consultant	
Child Care	
1. Entertaining children	1. Entertaining children
	2. Feeding children
	3. Dressing children
	4. Bathing children
Household Responsibilities	
1. Taking out trash	1. Cleaning house

2. Washing dishes

2. Washing clothes
3. Washing dishes
4. Cooking meals

Repair and Maintenance
1. Washing the car
2. Mowing the lawn
3. Repairing the car
4. Repairing the house
5. Repairing other items

1. Repairing misc. items

The next step is to exchange lists and estimate the amount of time each of your spouse's responsibilities demands from him/her each week: How many hours does your husband spend working as a financial consultant, mowing the lawn, and washing dishes each week? Have your husband estimate how many hours you spend bathing the children, cleaning the house, and cooking meals. Write the number of hours (15.00, .25, 1.75, etc.) each activity takes each week and total the numbers. (You both may be surprised by what these totals indicate!)

Next, exchange lists again and review the numbers to see if they fairly represent the time you each actually spend on the activities. Make any necessary adjustments. Then, again working with your spouse's list, write how much time you would like your spouse to spend on each activity: Would you like him to be spending more time entertaining the children and less time working in the yard? Would he like you to spend less time cleaning the house and more time just being with the children? With this give-and-take, you two are attempting to arrive at a total number of hours that is equitable for both of you. With some serious discussion, the art of compromise, and some adjustments, you'll be able to come up with a workable and equitable division of labor for your family and home.

One last comment. Couples face very real challenges when it comes to managing a home and raising a family when both husband and wife work outside the home. In fact, many women across America are deciding to stop working outside the home and to become full-time homemakers and mothers. They are realizing that's the only way that they can have the kind of home—and children!—they want to have. And being at home allows that home to be the castle a man wants and a haven of quietness, tranquillity, love, and acceptance that every family member needs.

5. Admiration

Men need sexual fulfillment, recreational companionship, an attractive spouse, domestic support, and, finally, admiration. People have very fragile identities. Men especially will go to great lengths to protect who they are as men. They must come to deeply trust a person before they will share who they really are. These facts make a man a sponge for admiration from his wife.

And, in all of the healthy marriages I have ever seen, the wife sincerely admires her husband—and she doesn't keep it a secret from him or anyone else! And such admiration could be the fifth "A" in the marriage seminar I do called "The Four A's: Acceptance—Adoration—Approval—Appreciation." When we husbands receive these things from our wives, we can be confident leaders in the home, capable providers, and the men of God He calls us to be.

Your husband truly needs your admiration and approval, and the Scriptures call you to give that to him: "If you love someone . . . you will always believe in him, always expect the best from him" (1 Corinthians 13:7 TLB). Wives, you need to be a cheerleader for your husband. Like our daughter, Jenny, who was a cheerleader from junior-high school days through her college years, you need to yell, scream, jump, and clap for that home team. When was the last time you cheered for your husband?

It's important that you let your husband know—beyond a shadow of a doubt—that he is your super-man, hero, and knight in shining armor. You can do this with a phone call or personal note which says, "You are special to me! I love you and I believe in you." Make a love basket or plan a weekend kidnapping. These acts of love release your husband to become all God wants him to be. And this kind of admiration encourages, energizes, and motivates your husband. It also helps him stand strong against the pressures and criticisms that may come with work.

We have heard that behind every great man is a great woman. A loving, admiring, and godly woman will indeed cause a man to gain greater stature than if he were on his own. A wife's encouragement can make her husband a better man, and that gift of encouragement can be evident quite early in life....

When our grandson Chad was six years old and competing on the local swim team, he finished last in an event. Seeing this, his little six-year-old friend Megan rushed to the edge of the pool and said excitedly, "Chad, you came in last, but you looked good!" This young girl was already being a cheerleader for the men in her life! Another woman was not quite as aware....

One day a repairman came to our home to repair our malfunctioning dishwasher. During my conversation with him, I learned that he was a new Christian who, after being involved in alcohol and drugs, was very excited about the Lord and about his new church. I also learned that his wife didn't like his church and was attending a different one. The repairman was discouraged. He wanted her to attend his church with him. I thought to myself, "This Christian woman doesn't understand her role as a wife!"

Admire your husband! Support him in his work and his play! Encourage him in his Christian walk! Shower him with acceptance, adoration, approval, and appreciation! Heed the anonymous but wise old saying, "Treat me as I am and that's just where I will stay. Treat me as if I were what I could be and that's what I'll become." Your man wants you, his wife, to be his most enthusiastic fan. He becomes stronger and more confident from your support and encouragement.

Your Husband's Needs

Standing by your man's needs is easier when you clearly understand what those needs are. I hope this chapter has given you some insight into your man and motivated you to meet his very real—but maybe not always spoken—needs. Your husband needs sexual fulfillment, recreational companionship, an attractive spouse, domestic support, and your admiration. Meet these needs, and you'll strengthen your husband *and* your marriage. And I can almost guarantee that you'll find your husband more interested in meeting your needs and more effective in doing so.

7

Stand by Your Man's Differences

And God created man in His own image,
in the image of God he created him;
male and female, He created them.

Genesis 1:27

Although the world with its unisex fashions and equal rights movements loudly argues that there are no differences between the sexes, those of us who are married know otherwise! It's evident to Emilie and me (as it should be to every husband and wife) that men and women are different—and those differences are much deeper than the obvious physical ones. What circumstances have caused you to realize just how differently you and your husband think? What situations have brought to the foreground the differences between how you and your husband act? Despite what the world says, men and women are different.

The world, though, invites women to expect men to think and act just as they do. In a marriage, these unrealistic expectations can result in disappointment and cries of "What's wrong with our marriage? He doesn't even care!" Are you sure your husband doesn't care? That may not be the case at all. You may simply have come up against the fact that a man will show that he cares differently than you, a woman, will show that you care. And how we express our love is just one of the many differences between men and women. What can a good wife do in the face of these differences? She can stand by her man, acknowledging and accepting how he is different from her.

Such acceptance comes more easily when we remember, first, that God made man and woman different. We also need to be aware that some of the differences are due to our individual strengths and weaknesses. You and your husband each entered into marriage with certain strengths and certain weaknesses. As a young man, I knew that I wanted a wife who would complement me—who would be strong where I was weak. When I met Emilie, I soon fell in love with her because she possessed certain traits that would complement or complete my weaknesses. And she continues to complement me. When people ask me if I'm threatened by Emilie's writing, speaking engagements, and expertise in time management and home organization, I reply, "No, because I am not in competition with Emilie. We complement each other." Likewise, I encourage you not to be threatened by differences between you and your husband. Instead, let those differences help make you a more complete person.

Too often, male-female differences are at the root of marital problems. This friction is due, though, not so much to the fact that men and women are physically, emotionally, psychologically, and culturally different from one another but from the fact that we don't understand those differences and work to accommodate them in our relationships. In contrast, a marriage grows and thrives when a husband and wife understand and accept that God has designed them to be different and complementary.

Physical Differences

Physical differences are the most obvious differences between men and women, but they are not the differences that cause the most friction in marriage. Nevertheless, understanding that God made men and women different physically is important when two lives are blended into one. Let's look at some of the physical differences between men and women:

- Women live an average of eight years longer than men.
- Men are usually stronger than women and able to run faster and lift more weight than women.
- Men have XY and XX chromosomes; women have XX chromosomes.
- The greater amount of the hormone testosterone in men increases their tendency toward aggression and physical activity.
- Men lose weight faster than women due to the lower ratio of muscle to fat.
- Men have a higher metabolic rate than women.
- A man's blood gives off more oxygen than a woman's.
- Women have greater endurance over the long haul than men.

- A woman's capacity to exercise is reduced two percent every 10 years whereas a man's capacity is reduced 10 percent over the same period.
- Men are performance-oriented in sexual intercourse; orgasm is the goal. Women are more interested in closeness and communication in sex, and they will trade physical sex for being held, caressed, and talked to.
- Men must be physically aroused for sex; women don't need physical arousal.
- A man's skin wrinkles later in life than a woman's skin.
- Our brains function differently. The male is more left-hemisphere controlled (logical) and the woman is more right-hemisphere controlled (intuitive, emotional).
- Men and women are anatomically different. The man's pelvis is narrow; the women's pelvis is broad for childbearing.

Again, these differences do not usually pose significant challenges to the marriage relationship, but they do underscore the fact that God made us, male and female, quite different from one another.

Psychological Differences

Far more significant in a marriage than physical differences are the psychological differences between men and women. It is interesting to note that these differences are rooted in physical differences—in the construction of the brain and the way it works. In *What Every Woman Should Know about Men*, Dr. Joyce Brothers offers the following background information:

> The fetus has what scientists call a "bipotential and undifferentiated brain," which means it can go either way (male or female)

depending on the influence of sex hormones. The brain is divided into a left and right hemisphere. The left (the verbal brain) controls language and reading skills. We use it when we balance our checkbook, read a newspaper, sing a song, play bridge, write a letter . . . The right hemisphere . . . is the center of our spatial abilities. We use it when we consult a road map, thread our way through a maze, work a jigsaw puzzle, design a house plan or plant a garden.[1]

Doreen Kimura elaborates on the differences between the male and female brain in her article from *Psychology Today*:

Sexual differences in the way the brain is organized suggest different ways of thinking and learning. The male brain is specialized. He uses one side for solving spatial problems, the other side for defining a word or verbalizing a problem. The female brain is not so specialized for some functions such as defining words. A woman's right-brain and left-brain abilities are duplicated to some extent in each hemisphere and work together to solve problems.[2]

If your husband is anything like me, he has a difficult time doing more than one or two things at a time. You are probably like Emilie, though, and able to work very effectively on three, four, or even five things at a time. Women can shift from right brain to left brain very quickly, and many times you rely on both hemispheres at the same time. Not us men! We have to come to a screeching halt in the left brain before we shift to the right brain. There is nothing wrong with us men. We're just different from you. That's how God created our brains to work!

This data on right brain and left brain explains several psychological differences between men and women.

- Women can better sense the difference between what people say and what they mean.
- Women are more perceptive than men about the meaning of feelings.
- Men have difficulty understanding women's intuition, often thinking that women are too sensitive.
- Women are more perceptive about people than men are.
- Men and women think differently and approach problem-solving differently. Men are more analytical and deal with the problem more objectively. Women are less objective; they personally identify with the problem.
- And, as mentioned earlier, women can work on several projects at once. Men want to concentrate on only one thing at a time.[3]

As you review this list, what differences do you encounter most frequently in your marriage? Has this list helped you better understand why certain points of tension exist between you and your husband? Some of the psychological differences you two run up against may be based in God-given physical differences. Being educated about these differences will help you both live with them—and with each other!

Cultural Differences

The physical and psychological differences between men and women give rise to several cultural differences, although it is sometimes difficult to determine where the unlearned hormonal differences leave off and the learned cultural differences begin. Consider the following discussion of marriage, commitment, and success in the business world.

In *Why Men Are the Way They Are,* author Warren Farrell states that men are performers who feel they must have an acceptable level of production to be fulfilled. As a performer, a man is competitive and goal-oriented. As an initiator, he is vulnerable to risk and failure and, as a result, often defensive in his relationships—even with his wife. Long-term relationships are risky for a man because they call him to expose his weaknesses, making him vulnerable to great hurt and possible defeat. Instead of moving closer to his woman, a man will defend himself from hurt and defeat by escaping the relationship. If he doesn't stay, his wife cannot hurt him or prove him to be a failure when it comes to marriage. (Statistics show that men are more apt to leave their marriages than women, and this background information suggests one reason why.) To compensate if not insure against failure in his relationships, a man works hard to succeed in business. After all, he rationalizes, if he is successful in the working world, he can buy whatever he needs to raise his sense of identity to a level he can live with, even if he is not successful on the home front. Success at work protects many men from the pain of their failure at home.[4]

A man's pursuit of success in business often produces characteristics which make him unlovable at home. When I was working on my master's degree and trying to get a mobile home business off the ground, I was not always pleasant to live with—as Emilie and the children will tell you. Emilie thought I should value the things she valued (home-life, child-raising, etc.), but I was busy—perhaps too busy at times—making my mark on the world. Emilie did not always understand my desire for success and approval on the job.

Our culture encourages this drive for success and holds up many other standards for "real" men to achieve. When husbands and wives address the culture's expectations of a man, they can avoid several sources of conflict. Which of the following ideas from today's culture are seeds of conflict in your marriage?

- The man is to be the breadwinner in the family. If his wife works, he feels that he is less than a real man.
- Men don't quit until they are carried off the field.
- Being "macho" is important. A man must be in shape, drive the right car, and belong to the right country club.
- Men must know about "men things"—boats, trucks, planes, cars, sports, etc.
- Men always read masculine magazines and never look at women's magazines.
- A man can perform sexually under any circumstances, on demand, and repeatedly.

The items listed seem based on learned cultural differences rather than unlearned hormonal differences, but it's not always easy to determine which is which.

Consider now that you are basically relationship-oriented while your husband is task- and success-oriented. (By the way, do you think this is learned or unlearned or a little of both?) When a man comes home after a busy day, he has already accomplished what he feels is really important: He has won the battles at the shop, office, or store and provided for his family. He wants to relax, watch television, and read the paper. His wife, however, has waited all day for him and is excited that he is home. He's ready to kick back, but she's ready to kick into gear! She wants to talk!

And talking is far more important to women than it is to men. As you know, you want your husband to share his deepest feelings and most intimate thoughts as well as the events of his day. You want to hear what he has to say, what he's thinking, and what he's feeling, and you want him to listen to you and try to understand what you're feeling. You want to be more than cleaning lady, cook, nursemaid, and child-care coordinator for your husband. You want to share in your man's life. You want a relationship based on communication and intimacy.

In her book *In a Different World*, Carol Gilligan summarizes the tension caused by the male's orientation toward tasks and the female's orientation toward relationships: "Since masculinity is defined through separation while femininity is defined through attachment, male gender identity is threatened by intimacy while female general identity is threatened by separation. Thus, males tend to have difficulty with relationships while females tend to have difficulty with individualization."[5]

In the academic world, the question again arises: How much of this—task-orientation versus relationship-orientation—is due to unlearned hormonal differences and how much to learned cultural differences? The article "Sexism in Our Schools—Training Girls for Failure?" raises questions about learned cultural differences between males and females. What do the following statistics say to you?

- Girls start school with higher test scores than boys. By the time they take the SAT as juniors in high school, girls trail boys by 57 points.

- In coed colleges, women speak up in class 2.5 times less often than their male classmates.

- After the first year of college, women show sharper drops in self-confidence than men do. The longer women stay in school, the lower their self-confidence falls.

- Women receive fewer than 17 percent of all the doctorates awarded in math and physics.

- A mere 10 percent of all high-school principals are women—a smaller percentage than in the 1950s.

- Only 11 percent of all full professors are women.

In her article, Conroy also presents data showing that teachers interact more with boys at every grade level, and it doesn't matter whether the teacher is male or female. The classroom scales tilt firmly in favor of boys but not because teachers deliberately exclude girls. Most teachers aren't even aware that they treat boys and girls differently, yet studies clearly show that they do. Here's what research reveals:

Feedback. Teachers praise boys far more often that they praise girls. Boys also receive more criticism. The benefits? Boys receive more encouragement and more chances to improve. They also learn how to handle criticism.

Attention. Boys call out for teacher attention eight times more often than girls—and boys receive it. When they speak out of turn in discussions, teachers accept the remarks as contributions. When girls do the same, teachers tell them to raise their hands.

Instruction. When students need help, teachers give the boys more detailed directions, but actually do the work for the girls. Thus, boys learn to be competent and girls learn to be helpless.

Literature. Children's books still portray a lopsided view of the world. In those that have won the prestigious Caldecott Medal, ten boys are pictured for every girl.

Course Selection. Schools still discourage girls from taking math, science, computer, and vocational classes, according to the Project on Equal Education Rights of the Legal Defense and Education Fund of the National Organization for Women.

Remedial Assistance. Girls don't get special help for learning or behavior disorders until they are older and further behind in school than boys with similar disabilities.[6]

Yes, there are cultural differences in our schools, and these differences create tension, at a very early age, between the sexes.

Besides the primary cultural differences of task- and relationship-orientation, several other cultural differences between men and women—often framed from childhood—shape our role expectations in marriage:

- Boys are supposed to be big, tough, and active while girls are tiny, sweet, and passive.
- Boys should play with trucks, guns, and trains while girls should choose dolls.

- Mothers are more affectionate with girls than boys. Boys are fussier than girls, and girls sleep better than boys.
- Boys are trained to be independent and girls are trained to be compliant.
- Boys are competitive and girls are cooperative.
- Boys form in small groups and gangs. Girls develop one-on-one relationships.
- Boys play softball and tell war stories in the locker room. Girls have tea parties and share personal, intimate conversation.
- Girls pattern themselves after their mothers, but boys don't want to copy feminine traits because they fear they will look like sissies around boys.[7]

Where do you see differences between the male culture and female culture causing tension in your marriage? How can understanding the source of some of the differences between you and your husband help you minimize the stress they cause?

Sexual Differences

Our society fosters cultural differences between men and women. God Himself, though, created us physically different, psychologically different, and—as we'll look at now—sexually different. As a young man of 22, however, I thought that men and women shared that excitement and were very much alike in their approach to love and sex. We men move easily from the wow! of being attracted to a woman to wanting to be sexual with her. Love comes later. Most women, however, are first attracted to a man and then they move to feelings of love. Wanting to be sexual with him comes later when she can trust him. Both men and women need to be aware of differences like this or we will never have our sexual needs met.

When I married Emilie, I learned firsthand about these differences between men and women. I saw quite clearly that women don't approach love the same way, and I quickly realized that what Emilie desired most in marriage was love, not sex. She desired sexual fulfillment, too, but she—like most women—viewed sex as a by-product of love. While a man grows in his love for his wife through sexual fulfillment, a woman finds sexual fulfillment when she is sure of her husband's love.

Also, men can usually become sexually aroused by visual or physical stimulation from any woman who is sexually available. It is easy for a man to engage in sex outside of love. Women, on the other hand, are generally more emotionally oriented. Though capable of being intensely erotic, a woman usually responds sexually to a man who provides her with security, understanding, tenderness, and compassion. Women who have extramarital affairs tend to do so because they are angry, lonely, insecure, or somehow unfulfilled in their marriage relationship. They receive the understanding or compassion they long for from someone other than their husband.

These differences between men and women came to light early in our marriage, as they undoubtedly did in yours. As a healthy, red-blooded male, my love for Emilie was first physically oriented. I expected that she, like me, was easily aroused sexually and that the sex act was a primary focus for her. But when I realized that she placed more value on love, affection, and romance, I had to slow down and make sure I was meeting those needs for her. When I learned how to assure Emilie of my love for her in nonsexual ways, sexual fulfillment came more easily for both of us.

I summarize this basic male/female difference

graphically with the following triangles:

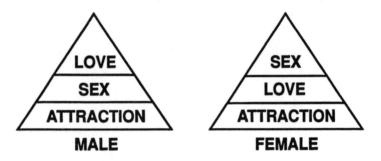

These triangles show that men move easily from being powerfully attracted to a woman to being ready for sex to (perhaps) falling in love. In contrast, most women move slowly from being attracted to a man to falling in love with him to then being ready to share with him sexually. In general, women need to feel in love and loved before they share themselves sexually. We men don't have to experience feelings of love. We have an easier time being ready to share sexually—and I know that women struggle to understand that about us.

And that's just one fact about how you women differ from us men when it comes to your sexuality that has become very clear to me through the years. I've also learned the following:

- You love to be romanced with flowers, a note, a box of candy, or suggestions of intimacy.
- You like to be talked to while making love—to be told how your husband is feeling and what he wants. Conversation builds intimacy and excitement.
- You like to take your time when being loved, and you take longer than us men to become fully aroused sexually.

- You need to feel emotionally secure in order to become fully aroused sexually.
- You want your husband to respect your body.
- You need patient and gentle attention as well as verbal appreciation.

Now you probably didn't learn much from that list. Do you know, though, how your husband differs from you when it comes to sexual fulfillment?

- Sex makes men feel wanted. Sex is a way for men to be received or accepted physically and emotionally.
- Men want to know they are doing a good job in life. Any constructive criticism needs to be expressed with love and tenderness.
- Men like women who like sex.
- Men like women who have a sense of humor.
- Men like to experience the feminine side of women.

What have you learned about your husband from this discussion of sexual differences? How can you stand by him despite the ways he differs from you sexually?

Created Differently

Men and women—as different as we are from one another physiologically, psychologically, emotionally, and sexually—are made in God's image (Genesis 1:27), and God called this creation good. A Christian husband and wife can be confident that God has put males and females on the earth for a special purpose and that our differences are by His design.

And Jesus Himself offers us the fundamental guidelines for how to respond to these differences. In Matthew 22:37-39, He simply and directly states the greatest commandments in the Scriptures: "You shall love the Lord your God with all your heart, and with all your soul, and with all your mind" and "You shall love your neighbor as yourself."

First, we are to love God, and part of loving God is honoring His creation—including the male-female differences built into that creation—as good. You must accept what God has made us: a unique man or woman created for a special purpose. Second, we are to love others, particularly the mate God has given us. Loving your husband doesn't mean changing him— that's the Holy Spirit's role. Loving your husband means understanding how he is different from you and accepting him as he is. I think that one of the lessons of Proverbs 24:3—"By wisdom a house is built, and by understanding it is established"— is that a loving understanding of one another as husband and wife establishes your marriage and your family. Continuously seeking to understand one another leads to less anger and frustration in a relationship. You may still be irritated, frustrated, or disturbed by your mate's actions, but at least you will be growing in your understanding of why he is doing what he's doing.

In Romans 12:2, the apostle Paul offers another scriptural guideline for dealing with differences in our marriages: "Do not be conformed to this world, but be transformed by the renewing of your mind, that you may prove what the will of God is, that which is good and acceptable and perfect." The world teaches us to stand up for our individuality and not to give in or accommodate another person's—even your mate's— different views or desires. We followers of Christ are to be different, though. We are to let God transform us "by the renewing of our minds" and so blend the differences between our thoughts and actions as He makes two truly become one.

Our Creator God has created us men and women, distinct and very different from one another. When we accept those differences as God-given and even blessed by Him, we will experience the rewards of more positive attitudes, better relationships, mutual respect, and a more godly character. We have a choice. We can live in a war zone fueled by our differences as men and women. Or we can live in a house filled with the precious and pleasant riches which come from understanding and accepting the differences that exist between us and our spouse (Proverbs 24:4). Perhaps the greatest enemy of such understanding and acceptance is pride. That's where God's transforming touch—referred to by Paul in Romans 12—can change our hearts and make us willing and able to offer love and acceptance to a spouse who is fundamentally and sometimes dramatically different from us.

Delightfully Different

We can be fundamentally and dramatically different from our mate—and Emilie and I are. We've experienced the entire gamut of differences discussed in this chapter. We also, though, have learned to see ourselves as delightfully different from one another. Despite different backgrounds and all the physical, emotional, and cultural differences discussed in this chapter, there has never been an air of competition between us. We have always wanted to complement each other. We are committed to Christ as the foundation of our home and our relationship. I am committed to loving Emilie as Christ loved the church, and she is dedicated to being my helpmate and to reverencing me as her husband. These points of agreement enable us to overcome our differences, and, in response to our prayers, God is able to use us to His glory in spite of our differences.

Early on in our marriage, I was locked into the world's macho-tainted expectations of men. I had tunnel vision regarding the home, children, God, and church. I was typically oriented toward such masculine endeavors as job satisfaction and career goals. I've had to work to move away from a tendency to conform to the world in those areas. Instead of accepting what the world said a man should be, I had to open myself to moving in a godly direction. Romans 12:2 alerted me not to be conformed to the role for a husband that the world defined, but to be transformed to God's definition of marital roles. I realized that if Emilie and I were going to have a healthy marriage and family life, I needed to shatter the worldly mold which threatened to shape me into its mold.

As I searched the Scriptures (especially the book of Ephesians), I discovered lessons I've shared with you. I learned that Emilie and I were both made for the purpose of worshiping and enjoying God; that we had each been wonderfully created with unique male or female characteristics; that we weren't to be abrasive to one another in our differences; and that we were, with God's blessing, to complement one other according to His plan. God's Word helped me see marriage afresh and to understand His design for this institution. Every question I had regarding our differences was answered by Scripture. I simply needed to study and apply the truth to my life.

While I was discovering my scriptural role in the home, Emilie was growing too. God was preparing her to share with other women what she was learning about the wife's role in marriage. As each of us got to know God better through studying His Word, we got to know each other better, too. Gradually our differences and inadequacies became less effective instruments in

Satan's attempt to weaken our marriage and neutralize our ministry.

Emilie and I had some help along the way, though, and this help is available to you. First, I highly recommend to you Dr. Tim LaHaye's book *The Spirit-Controlled Temperament* as a tool for you and your husband to work through your differences. Second, the ministry of Fred and Florence Littauer helped us examine our personal strengths and weaknesses and then accentuate the positive and eliminate the negative. It also helped us understand that people who are different from us, including our spouses, are not wrong—they're just different. When we realize that others can be different from us without being wrong, our relationships improve. After all, God created each of us to be unique, and our uniqueness adds spice to life as we see things from different points of view.

Also, once we examine ourselves and stop trying to change our spouse, we find ourselves open to God's gentle and transforming touch (Romans 12:2). Yes, you—as I did and still do—have a choice. You can be conformed to this world or transformed to God's point of view. Emilie and I know hundreds of couples who have chosen the latter alternative. With them, we recommend that you don't let your differences move you to a relational war zone. Instead, let God use those differences to lift you to new heights in your relationship. Emilie and I have found that our differences have indeed led to a richer and more meaningful relationship, not only for ourselves. May God be with you as you learn to appreciate the differences that exist between you and your husband. And may those differences actually become elements of cement in your relationship, giving new life, spice, and adventure to your marriage. As Emilie and I often say, don't compete—complete! Stand by your man even though he is very different from you!

8

Stand by Your Man's Temperament

Thou didst form my inward parts;
Thou didst weave me in my mother's womb.

Psalm 139:13

ave you ever thought about the fact that, in the words of a speaker I heard once, "Men are weird and women are strange"?[1] I know that I find Emilie really strange in many areas of her life! For starters, she genuinely likes to clean house, sweep leaves off the sidewalks, iron pillowcases, decorate our home, and play with the grandchildren for hours on end. She also gets quite excited if I don't apply the brakes a hundred feet before I come to stopped traffic. Pretty strange, wouldn't you say?

At the same time, though, Emilie is well aware that

I'm weird. As evidence, she points to the fact that, on a trip, I won't take the scenic route, stop to go to the restroom, or let another car pass me because I've got to get wherever we're going first. She also doesn't understand why, when I run an errand, I leave the store with only the one or two items that were on my list. She sees these behaviors as weird!

As if physical, psychological, cultural, and sexual differences weren't challenge enough to overcome in a marriage, most husbands and wives have to deal with yet another critical difference—a difference in temperament. In the preceding chapter, I mentioned how the work of Tim and Beverly LaHaye and Fred and Florence Littauer have helped Emilie and me understand ourselves and each other and so bridge the gap between our personalities.

Differences like the ones I mentioned above really bothered Emilie and me until we learned about temperaments and recognized how fundamentally different we are from each other. At the same time, we learned the important truth that neither of us is wrong—we are simply different from one another. We also learned that people often marry someone with a temperament opposite their own. One reason God gives us such a partner is to provide us with a mate who can be strong where we are weak. I know that I am a much stronger person today because Emilie brought into our marriage her strengths that complemented my weaknesses and therefore made them strong. Emilie's friendliness, for instance, has helped me become more open to people. But regardless of the good that comes out of temperament differences, the fact remains that dealing with them can be tough. Before looking closely at temperament differences, it's important to recognize that "different" does not imply superior/inferior, better/worse, or right/wrong and that, in fact, differences can mean strength.

The Two Shall Become One

As one of Aesop's fables communicates so well, understanding and accepting temperament differences is well worth the effort. According to the famed story-teller, a wise father sensed disharmony among his sons and decided to bring them together to discuss this strife. He told each of his four sons to bring a twig to the meeting.

As the young men assembled, the father took each boy's twig and easily snapped it in half. Then, as they watched, he gathered four twigs, tied them together in a bundle, and asked each son to try to break the bundle. Each one tried to no avail. The bundle would not snap.

After each son had tried valiantly to break the bundle, the father asked his boys what they had learned from the demonstration. The oldest son said, "If we are individuals, anyone can break us, but if we stick togeth-er, no one can harm us." The father said, "You are right. You must always stand together and be strong."

What is true for the four brothers is equally true for a husband and wife. If we don't stand together and let God make us one despite our temperament differ-ences, we will easily be defeated. Furthermore, the Bible calls us to such oneness. Genesis 2:24 states, "A man shall leave his father and his mother, and shall cleave to his wife; and they shall become one flesh." God first showed me this verse more than a year before I met Emilie. He had given me a real desire to marry and raise a family, and I knew He was at work preparing me to share my life with a very special woman. At that point, however, I had no idea who that woman would be or what Genesis 2:24 really meant.

But as I studied that verse, I saw God calling a husband and wife to

- departure ("A man shall leave his father and mother . . ."),
- permanence ("And shall cleave to his wife . . ."), and
- oneness ("And they shall become one flesh").

And these three steps must be taken if a marriage is to stand strong despite the different temperaments of the two people involved.

• *Departure*—Besides physically leaving their parents' homes, both the husband and wife are to become emotionally and financially independent as well. The marriage relationship—and the new family that has been created—is to be the primary source of emotional health, financial provision, security, and protection. The new couple will not make an absolute break from their parents, but they must realize that they are now a family and that they need to make their own decisions. The new husband and wife must have greater loyalty to one another than to their parents.

Such departing wasn't difficult for Emilie or for me. Emilie's father died during her childhood, so there was no tie to break with him. Since she was to remain geographically close to her mother after our marriage, Emilie's separation from her did not prove to be a hardship. Like Emilie, I also didn't struggle to leave my family. Midway through college, I had moved out of my parents' home and became a live-in caretaker for the estate of a very wealthy family. My parents had raised all three of their sons so that we were ready to leave the home as young men, and I was.

This kind of physical move from the parents' home is just one kind of departure necessary in a healthy marriage. Husbands and wives also need to depart emotionally. Too many married adults are still controlled by parents because they have never consciously stepped away from their emotional control. The process of stepping away emotionally will be gradual, and that process is harder when strong, controlling parents are involved. In that case, the departing young adult may be made to feel guilty about leaving, but such emotional separation is necessary and healthy. It doesn't mean that we no longer care about our parents. It simply means that we are not under parental control.

Financial independence is another important aspect of leaving home. Leaving financially means we are free to accept financial assistance from our parents, but we no longer depend on them for the funds we need. Again, many adults have not tried to achieve financial independence because they are waiting for an inheritance from their parents. These people have never taken responsibility for their own financial situation because they are counting on Dad and Mom's money to be there for them—as it always has been.

Achieving independence from one's parents can be a long or short, an easy or a difficult process. Perhaps, to make it easier on young people as well as their parents, we Christians should follow the example of our Jewish brothers and sisters. In the Jewish wedding ceremonies we've attended, parents of both the bride and groom recite vows releasing their children from their authority. Formally releasing one's children could serve to eliminate a lot of uncertainty, guilt, and unhealthy dependence as a new couple works to get established. Again, departure doesn't mean that parents and their married children will never see each other. It does mean a new phase of the relationship in which parents regard their grown children as independent adults capable of managing their own home, their own emotional lives, and their own financial situations.

As I look at many couples today, though, I often observe with great sadness that one or both marriage partners have not made this crucial break from Mom and Dad. You, as a wife, cannot freely give to your husband until you know in your heart that you are more important to him than any other person in his life. Likewise, a husband needs to know that he is the most important person in your life before he can be fully committed to you. We show our spouse that he/she holds that number one spot when, at every level, we do indeed leave our parents' house.

• *Permanence.* According to Genesis 2:24, leaving one's father and mother is just the first step toward a strong and godly marriage. Next, the verse states, a man "shall cleave to his wife." The Hebrew word translated "cleave" means "to cling" or "to be glued to" and clearly expresses God's intention that a husband and wife be bonded to one another permanently. Marriage is not an experiment or a trial run. Marriage is a once-and-for-all union.

In light of the fact that marriage should be permanent, God gives these instructions to a newly married couple: "When a man takes a new wife, he shall not go out with the army, nor be charged with any duty; he shall be free at home one year and shall give happiness to his wife whom he has taken" (Deuteronomy 24:5). The Hebrew bridegroom was commanded to set his responsibilities aside for one year and concentrate on making his wife happy. This period of time gave the couple the opportunity to get to know one another and build a foundation for a marriage that would last.

Few newlyweds today have available the resources

that would allow them to quit their jobs and spend every moment of their first year alone together. But there are some practical steps all married couples can take to apply or reinforce the glue of permanence in their marriage.

Leave your parents' homes and set up a home of your own. If at all possible, do not live in the same house with either of your parents even if it is more economical to do so.

Spend as much time together as possible. Your marriage is to take priority over nights out with the girls and hunting, fishing, or bowling with the boys. After all, we can't build a relationship with our spouse that will last if we don't spend time together, especially when we're first married. Our spouses are more important than our friends, and our actions need to reflect that fact even if old friends don't understand.

Reserve the bedroom for sleeping and loving—and do this by keeping the television out of your bedroom. Many husbands go to bed to see the end of a movie, the late news, or the last play of the ball game. When this happens, the television robs many couples of the happiness they should be providing each other in the bedroom.

Permanence isn't valued in our culture today, but it's valued by our God, the One who established marriage for us. Furthermore, permanence doesn't happen automatically. It takes work—but the rewards make the work well worth the effort.

• *Oneness.* After calling husbands and wives to leave their fathers and mothers and cleave to one another, God says that the two "shall become one flesh" (Genesis 2:24). In God's sight, we become one at the altar when we say our vows to one another before Him, but practically speaking, oneness between a husband and wife is a process that happens over a period of time—over their lifetime together.

Becoming one with another person can be a very difficult process. It isn't easy to change from being independent and self-centered to sharing every aspect of your life and self with another person. The difficulty is intensified when you're older and more set in your ways when you marry or, as was the case for Emilie and me, when the two partners come from very different family, religious, and financial backgrounds. Emilie, for instance, came from an alcoholic family and was raised by a verbally and physically abusive father. I came from a warm, loving family where yelling and screaming simply didn't happen. It took us only a few moments to say our vows and enter into oneness in God's eyes, but we have spent more than 37 years blending our lives and building the oneness which we enjoy today.

And let me explain that becoming one doesn't mean becoming the same. Oneness means sharing the same degree of commitment to the Lord and to the marriage, the same goals and dreams, and the same mission in life. Oneness is internal conformity to one another, not the external conformity of Marines with their short haircuts, muscular bodies, shiny shoes, straight backs, and characteristic walk. The oneness and internal conformity of a marriage relationship comes with the unselfish act of allowing God to shape us into the marriage partner He would have us be. Oneness results when two individuals reflect the same Christ. Such spiritual oneness produces tremendous strength and unity in a marriage and in the family.

Consider what Paul writes to the church at Philippi: "Make my joy complete by being of the same mind, maintaining the same love, united in spirit, intent on one purpose" (Philippians 2:2). This verse has guided me in my roles as husband and father. It has called me, as the leader, to work to unite my family in purpose, thought, and deed. After many years of trial, error, and endless hours of searching, I can say that we are united in our purpose and direction. If you were to ask Emilie to state our purpose and direction, her answer would match mine: The litmus test for us is Matthew 6:33—"Seek first His kingdom and His righteousness; and all these things shall be added to you." As we have faced decisions through the years, we have asked ourselves, "Are we seeking God's kingdom and His righteousness? Will doing this help us find His kingdom and experience His righteousness? Or are we seeking our own edification or our own satisfaction?" Emilie and I both hold this standard up whenever we have to decide an issue, and that oneness of purpose helps make our marriage work.

Larry Crabb points out another important dimension to the oneness of a husband and wife when he writes, "The goal of oneness can be almost frightening when we realize that God does not intend [only] that my wife and I find our personal needs met in marriage. He also wants our relationship to validate the claims of Christianity to a watching world as an example of the power of Christ's redeeming love to overcome the divisive effects of sin."[2]

The world does not value permanence and oneness in a marriage, and much of our culture works to undermine those characteristics. But knowing what God intends marriage to be, working to leave, cleave, and become one with our spouse, and understanding that our temperament differences can strengthen our unity with our mate—these things will help our marriages shine God's light in a very dark world.

Differences in Temperament

It doesn't take this chapter—or the LaHayes' and the Littauers' excellent and thorough work on temperaments—to tell you that your mate is different from you. You are well aware that your spouse doesn't react to situations, people, or life in general the same way you do. The reason is, simply, that God made your husband different from you. In fact, that difference is undoubtedly part of what made him attractive to you in the first place. Now, however, these differences may be a real source of irritation. They may even be affecting your love for each other. But that doesn't have to be the case. Temperament differences can instead be sources of strength and oneness, and the following discussion may help you bridge the differences and strengthen your marriage.

As Florence Littauer points out in *After Every Wedding Comes a Marriage*, the study of temperament differences goes way back:

> Four hundred years before Christ was born, Hippocrates first presented the concept of the temperaments to the world. As a physician and philosopher, he dealt closely with people and saw that there were extroverts and introverts, optimists and pessimists. He further categorized people according to their body fluids as Sanguine, blood; Choleric, yellow bile; Melancholy, black bile; and Phlegmatic, phlegm. While modern psychologists do not hold to the theory of the fluids, the terms and characteristics are still valid.[3]

While the terms today may vary (colors, animals, "Type A"/"Type B" may be used), psychologists agree

that human beings are divided into four basic personality groups—Sanguine, Melancholy, Choleric, and
Phlegmatic. The Littauers' Personality Profile (which
appears on the following pages and in many of their
writings) helps readers identify their temperament
type, identify their strengths and weaknesses, and so
better know themselves and one another.

At this point, let me add that it is important to look
at your weaknesses as well as your strengths. We all
proudly look at our strengths, but we aren't nearly as
thrilled to look at our weaknesses. Few of us like to
confront the negative aspects of our personalities (who
likes to hear that they are brassy, interruptive, frank,
manipulative, insecure, or moody?), but these nega-
tives can teach us much about ourselves. If our goal is
to know ourselves, then we must look into the mirror
and acknowledge our negative characteristics. Only
then will we be able to decide what to do about those
negative traits.

Take some time right now to work through the
Personality Profile.[4] After recording your strengths and
weaknesses on the first 40 lines, transfer your answers
to the Personality Scoring Sheets on pages 144 and 145
and see how your temperament traits are distributed.
You will probably find that most of your traits fall into
two categories, although some people will have traits
in all four areas. Which two classifications do most of
your personality traits fall under?

The most common combinations are Sanguine-
Cholerics, outgoing, optimistic people who make
excellent leaders, and Melancholy-Phlegmatics, cau-
tious, introverted folks who like quiet, reflective thinking. Temperament traits tend to fall evenly into the
categories paired here: half under "Sanguine" and half
under "Choleric," for example.

Personality Profile

DIRECTIONS—In each of the following rows of four words across, place an X in front of the one word that most often applies to you. Continue through all forty lines. Be sure each number is marked. If you are not sure of which word "most applies," ask a spouse or a friend.

STRENGTHS

#				
1	____ Adventurous	____ Adaptable	____ Animated	____ Analytical
2	____ Persistent	____ Playful	____ Persuasive	____ Peaceful
3	____ Submissive	____ Self-sacrificing	____ Sociable	____ Strong-willed
4	____ Considerate	____ Controlled	____ Competitive	____ Convincing
5	____ Refreshing	____ Respectful	____ Reserved	____ Resourceful
6	____ Satisfied	____ Sensitive	____ Self-reliant	____ Spirited
7	____ Planner	____ Patient	____ Positive	____ Promoter
8	____ Sure	____ Spontaneous	____ Scheduled	____ Shy
9	____ Orderly	____ Obliging	____ Outspoken	____ Optimistic
10	____ Friendly	____ Faithful	____ Funny	____ Forceful
11	____ Daring	____ Delightful	____ Diplomatic	____ Detailed
12	____ Cheerful	____ Consistent	____ Cultured	____ Confident
13	____ Idealistic	____ Independent	____ Inoffensive	____ Inspiring
14	____ Demonstrative	____ Decisive	____ Dry humor	____ Deep
15	____ Mediator	____ Musical	____ Mover	____ Mixes easily
16	____ Thoughtful	____ Tenacious	____ Talker	____ Tolerant
17	____ Listener	____ Loyal	____ Leader	____ Lively
18	____ Contented	____ Chief	____ Chartmaker	____ Cute
19	____ Perfectionist	____ Pleasant	____ Productive	____ Popular
20	____ Bouncy	____ Bold	____ Behaved	____ Balanced

Personality Profile

21	___ Blank	___ Bashful	___ Brassy	___ Bossy
22	___ Undisciplined	___ Unsympathetic	___ Unenthusiastic	___ Unforgiving
23	___ Reticent	___ Resentful	___ Resistant	___ Repetitious
24	___ Fussy	___ Fearful	___ Forgetful	___ Frank
25	___ Impatient	___ Insecure	___ Indecisive	___ Interrupts
26	___ Unpopular	___ Uninvolved	___ Unpredictable	___ Unaffectionate
27	___ Headstrong	___ Haphazard	___ Hard to please	___ Hesitant
28	___ Plain	___ Pessimistic	___ Proud	___ Permissive
29	___ Angered easily	___ Aimless	___ Argumentative	___ Alienated
30	___ Naive	___ Negative attitude	___ Nervy	___ Nonchalant
31	___ Worrier	___ Withdrawn	___ Workaholic	___ Wants credit
32	___ Too sensitive	___ Tactless	___ Timid	___ Talkative
33	___ Doubtful	___ Disorganized	___ Domineering	___ Depressed
34	___ Inconsistent	___ Introvert	___ Intolerant	___ Indifferent
35	___ Messy	___ Moody	___ Mumbles	___ Manipulative
36	___ Slow	___ Stubborn	___ Show-off	___ Skeptical
37	___ Loner	___ Lord over	___ Lazy	___ Loud
38	___ Sluggish	___ Suspicious	___ Short-tempered	___ Scatterbrained
39	___ Revengeful	___ Restless	___ Reluctant	___ Rash
40	___ Compromising	___ Critical	___ Crafty	___ Changeable

NOW TRANSFER ALL YOUR X's TO THE CORRESPONDING WORDS ON THE PERSONALITY SCORING SHEET AND ADD UP THE TOTALS.

Personality Scoring Sheet

	SANGUINE POPULAR	CHOLERIC POWERFUL	MELANCHOLY PERFECT	PHLEGMATIC PEACEFUL
1	Animated	Adventurous	Analytical	Adaptable
2	Playful	Persuasive	Persistent	Peaceful
3	Sociable	Strong-willed	Self-sacrificing	Submissive
4	Convincing	Competitive	Considerate	Controlled
5	Refreshing	Resourceful	Respectful	Reserved
6	Spirited	Self-reliant	Sensitive	Satisfied
7	Promoter	Positive	Planner	Patient
8	Spontaneous	Sure	Scheduled	Shy
9	Optimistic	Outspoken	Orderly	Obliging
10	Funny	Forceful	Faithful	Friendly
11	Delightful	Daring	Detailed	Diplomatic
12	Cheerful	Confident	Cultured	Consistent
13	Inspiring	Independent	Idealistic	Inoffensive
14	Demonstrative	Decisive	Deep	Dry humor
15	Mixes easily	Mover	Musical	Mediator
16	Talker	Tenacious	Thoughtful	Tolerant
17	Lively	Leader	Loyal	Listener
18	Cute	Chief	Chartmaker	Contented
19	Popular	Productive	Perfectionist	Pleasant
20	Bouncy	Bold	Behaved	Balanced
TOTALS	___	___	___	___

Personality Scoring Sheet

WEAKNESSES

	SANGUINE POPULAR	CHOLERIC POWERFUL	MELANCHOLY PERFECT	PHLEGMATIC PEACEFUL
21	Brassy	Bossy	Bashful	Blank
22	Undisciplined	Unsympathetic	Unforgiving	Unenthusiastic
23	Repetitious	Resistant	Resentful	Reticent
24	Forgetful	Frank	Fussy	Fearful
25	Interrupts	Impatient	Insecure	Indecisive
26	Unpredictable	Unaffectionate	Unpopular	Uninvolved
27	Haphazard	Headstrong	Hard-to-please	Hesitant
28	Permissive	Proud	Pessimistic	Plain
29	Angered easily	Argumentative	Alienated	Aimless
30	Naive	Nervy	Negative attitude	Nonchalant
31	Wants credit	Workaholic	Withdrawn	Worrier
32	Talkative	Tactless	Too sensitive	Timid
33	Disorganized	Domineering	Depressed	Doubtful
34	Inconsistent	Intolerant	Introvert	Indifferent
35	Messy	Manipulative	Moody	Mumbles
36	Show-off	Stubborn	Skeptical	Slow
37	Loud	Lord-over-others	Loner	Lazy
38	Scatterbrained	Short tempered	Suspicious	Sluggish
39	Restless	Rash	Revengeful	Reluctant
40.	Changeable	Crafty	Critical	Compromising
TOTALS				
COMBINED TOTALS				

Another standard combination is Melancholy-Choleric, denoting a strong and organized person who accomplishes much and really likes to work. Rather than falling evenly into these categories, 60 percent of your traits may fall into one category and 40 percent into the other. If 60 percent fall under "Choleric," you are probably more optimistic, directive, quick-moving, and able to organize ideas in your head. If 60 percent fall under "Melancholy," you may be somewhat pessimistic, quiet as you give direction, slower to move, and preferring to do your organizing on paper. (A high percentage of business executives are this Melancholy-Choleric combination.)

Like the Melancholy-Choleric personality, the Sanguine-Phlegmatic will tip more in one direction than the other. A mostly Sanguine person will be light-hearted, good-humored, easygoing, fun-loving, and optimistic. If the Phlegmatic prevails, a person will have a dry sense of humor and be quieter, slower-paced, and more laid back, giving the impression that he/she is not concerned about anything. Sanguine-Phlegmatics are always friendly, relaxed, and appealing people, but they can also be poor handlers of money. Also, believing that "all work and no play makes Jack a dull boy," they feel the tug-of-war between the two and may often be unable to get their career on track.

For a more complete discussion of these temperament types, see the descriptions on pages 147-154 by Florence Littauer. With an open mind and heart, read the two categories into which most of your traits fall. These summaries are not cast in concrete; they merely are an indication of your personality type, a benchmark to help you learn about yourself.

POPULAR SANGUINE SUMMARY
"Let's do it the fun way."

Desire:	Have fun.
Emotional Needs:	Attention, affection, approval, acceptance.
Key Strengths:	Can talk about anything at any time at any place with or without information. Has a bubbling personality, optimism, sense of humor, storytelling ability, likes people.
Key Weaknesses:	Disorganized, can't remember details or names, exaggerates, not serious about anything, trusts others to do the work, too gullible and naive.
Gets Depressed When:	Life is not fun and no one seems to love him.
Is Afraid of:	Being unpopular or bored, having to live by the clock or keep a record of money spent.
Likes People Who:	Listen and laugh, praise and approve.
Dislikes People Who:	Criticize, don't respond to his humor, don't think he is cute.

Is Valuable in Work: For colorful creativity, optimism, light touch, cheering up others, entertaining.

Could Improve If: He got organized, didn't talk so much and learned to tell time.

Tends to Marry: Perfects who are sensitive and serious, but the Populars quickly tire of having to cheer them up all the time and of being made to feel inadequate and stupid.

Reaction to Stress: Leave the scene, go shopping, find a fun group, create excuses, blame others.

Recognize by: Constant talking, loud volume, bright eyes, moving hands, colorful expressions, enthusiasm, ability to mix easily.

POWERFUL CHOLERIC SUMMARY
"Let's do it my way."

Desire:	Have control.
Emotional Needs:	Sense of obedience, appreciation for accomplishments, credit for ability.
Key Strengths:	Ability to take charge of anything instantly, make quick, correct judgments.
Key Weaknesses:	Too bossy, domineering, autocratic, insensitive, impatient, unwilling to delegate or give credit to others.
Gets Depressed When:	Life is out of control and people won't do things his way.
Is Afraid of:	Losing control of anything, such as losing job, not being promoted, becoming seriously ill, having a rebellious child or unsupportive mate.
Likes People Who:	Are supportive and submissive, see things his way, cooperate quickly and let him take credit.
Dislikes People Who:	Are lazy and not interested in working constantly, who buck his authority, get independent or aren't loyal.

Is Valuable in Work:	Because he can accomplish more than anyone else in a shorter time and is usually right, but may stir up trouble.
Could Improve If:	He allowed others to make decisions, delegated authority, became more patient, didn't expect everyone to produce as he does.
As a Leader He:	Has a natural feel for being in charge, a quick sense of what will work and a sincere belief in his ability to achieve, but may overwhelm less aggressive people.
Tends to Marry:	Peacefuls who will quietly obey and not buck his authority, but who never accomplish enough or get excited over his projects.
Reaction to Stress:	Tighten control, work harder, exercise more, get rid of offender.
Recognize by:	Fast-moving approach, quick grab for control, self-confidence, restless and overpowering attitude.

PERFECT MELANCHOLY SUMMARY
"Let's do it the right way."

Desire:	Have it right.
Emotional Needs:	Sense of stability, space, silence, sensitivity, and support.
Key Strengths:	Ability to organize, set long-range goals, have high standards and ideals, analyze deeply.
Key Weaknesses:	Easily depressed, too much time on preparation, too focused on details, remembers negatives, suspicious of others.
Gets Depressed When:	Life is out of order, standards aren't met and no one seems to care.
Is Afraid of:	No one understanding how he really feels, making a mistake, having to compromise standards.
Likes People Who:	Are serious, intellectual, deep, and will carry on a sensible conversation.
Dislikes People Who:	Are lightweights, forgetful, late, disorganized, superficial, prevaricating, and unpredictable.

Is Valuable in Work:

For sense of details, love of analysis, follow-through, high standards of performance, compassion for the hurting.

Could Improve If:

He didn't take life quite so seriously and didn't insist others be perfectionists.

As a Leader He:

Organizes well, is sensitive to people's feelings, has deep creativity, wants quality performance.

Tends to Marry:

Populars for their personalities and social skills, but soon tries to shut them up and get them on a schedule, becoming depressed when they don't respond.

Reaction to Stress:

Withdraws, gets lost in a book, becomes depressed, gives up, recounts the problems.

Recognize by:

Serious, sensitive nature, well-mannered approach, self-deprecating comments, meticulous and well-groomed looks (exceptions are hippie-type intellectuals, musicians, poets, who feel attention to clothes and looks is worldly and detracts from their inner strengths).

PEACEFUL PHLEGMATIC SUMMARY
"Let's do it the easy way."

Desire: Have no conflict, keep peace.

Emotional Needs: Sense of respect, feeling of worth, understanding, emotional support, harmony.

Key Strengths: Balance, even disposition, dry sense of humor, pleasing personality.

Key Weaknesses: Lack of decisiveness, enthusiasm and energy, but has no obvious flaws, and has a hidden will of iron.

Gets Depressed When: Life is full of conflict, he has to face a personal confrontation, no one wants to help, the buck stops with him.

Is Afraid of: Having to deal with a major personal problem, being left holding the bag, making major changes.

Likes People Who: Will make decisions for him, recognize his strengths, and not ignore him.

Dislikes People Who: Are too pushy, expect too much of him.

Is Valuable in Work: Because he cooperates and is a calming influence, keeps peace, mediates between contentious people, objectively solves problems.

Could Improve If: He sets goals and become self-motivated, he were willing to do more and move faster than expected, and could face his own problems as well as he handles other people's.

As a Leader He: Keeps calm, cool, and collected; doesn't make impulsive decisions, is well-liked and inoffensive, won't cause trouble, but doesn't come up with brilliant new ideas.

Tends to Marry: Powerfuls because they respect his strength and decisiveness, but later the Peacefuls get tired of being pushed around and looked down upon.

Reaction to Stress: Hide from it, watch TV, eat.

Recognize by: Calm approach, relaxed posture, sitting or leaning when possible.[5]

After carefully reading through the two descriptions which your Personality Profile suggested best fit you, spend some time thinking about what you've read. What do these overviews say to you about yourself? What can God teach you about yourself? Where do you think He would like you to work on becoming more Christlike? Also, ask your spouse or a trusted friend how accurately the descriptions fit you.

According to 1 Corinthians 11:28, we are to examine ourselves before we receive the Lord's Supper, but such self-examination can be beneficial at other times as well. When we look at ourselves, we can see where God would change us. We can also stop trying to change others and allow them to be different. When we allow our spouse to be different from us (and, again, different is not inferior or wrong), our marriage may definitely improve.

So stand by your man even though his temperament is different from yours. After all, God created each of us to be unique. Accept wholeheartedly those areas where your spouse is different from you. Learn from him. Offer your strengths where he is weak and let his strengths complement your weaknesses. A richer marriage will result!

9

Stand by Your Man as a Friend

It is not good for the man to be alone.

Genesis 2:18

Genesis 2:18-25 is a beautiful picture of how God created not only the first woman and wife, but also the first friend. A wife is indeed to be her husband's friend, and that has truly been my experience. Through the years, the love Emilie and I have for each other has grown, and we have become each other's best friend. The Genesis passage suggests that that is exactly what God intends for a married couple. Let's look closely at that section of Scripture.

• God gives the woman to the man to be "a helper suitable for him" (2:18). Do you consider yourself a helper or a hindrance to your husband? To his work? To his time at home? Are you "suitable" or unsuitable when it comes to recognizing and meeting his needs? Where could you be more helpful to him? If you're not sure, why not ask him?

• God creates woman from man's rib (2:21,22). Earlier in Genesis, we learn that God created human beings in His image (1:27). The fact that each of us is created in God's image calls us to honor and respect one another. Consider for a moment that your husband was made by God in His image, just as you were. How, then, should you treat him? Acknowledging that your husband has been created in the image of God calls you, I believe, to respect and honor him and to offer him love and friendship.

• Adam perceived Eve as part of his own bone and own flesh (2:23). If, like Adam, I rightly understand that Emilie is actually part of me, I will want to treat her as well as I treat myself. I will want to take good care of her and provide for her every need. This kind of husband love provides a good foundation for the kind of friendship a wife can give her man.

• Man is to leave his parents and cleave to his wife (2:24). As we saw in the preceding chapter, the two marriage partners must leave their families and let God make them one. We men help the cleaving happen when we show—not just tell—you, our wife, that you are our most important priority after God. Likewise, a wife needs to let her husband know how important he is to her. Your man cannot be competing with your father or any other male for the number one position in your life. He must know that you respect, honor, and love him if he is to act out his proper role as man, husband, and father. Besides building up your husband's confidence, your clear communication of your love for him will strengthen the bond of marriage.

• The man and the woman stood naked before each other and were not ashamed (2:25). When husbands and wives accept the first four principles—when we understand that we are created in God's image, when we husbands recognize that our wife is "bone of my bones, and flesh of my flesh" (2:23) and treat her as such, when a wife is a suitable helper to her man, and when spouses cleave to one another—husbands and wives can indeed stand before one another "naked and . . . not ashamed" (2:25). In fact, that phrase points to a fundamental aspect of true friendship. I don't think a married couple can explore the depths of friendship until they stand before each other naked—physically, emotionally, and psychologically. This openness provides a strong foundation for friendship. Consider the following definition of a friend.

> And what is a friend? Many things . . . A friend is someone you are comfortable with, someone whose company you prefer. A friend is someone you can count on—not only for support, but for honesty.
>
> A friend is one who believes in you . . . someone with whom you can share your dreams. In fact, a real friend is a person you want to share all of life with—and the sharing doubles the fun.
>
> When you are hurting and you can share your struggle with a friend, it eases the pain. A friend offers you safety and trust. . . . Whatever you say will never be used against you.
>
> A friend will laugh with you, but not at you. . . . A friend will pray with you . . . and for you.
>
> My friend is one who hears my cry of pain,

who senses my struggle, who shares my lows
as well as my highs.[1]

In such a friendship, nothing is hidden. Such
friendship is built on trust, and such friendship takes
time to grow and develop. What better context for this
kind of friendship to grow than your marriage? But
how does your marriage measure up against this
description? If you and your husband don't yet share
this kind of friendship, don't wait for him to reach out.
Take the initial step and see how he responds. If you
have tried before and not been well received, ask God
to guide and bless your efforts and then risk reaching
out again.

When Pain Is a Roadblock

Perhaps your friendship with your husband is
being blocked by some pain that you're dealing with.
Perhaps you find yourself in a tunnel of chaos (chapter
2) and unable to reach out to him as you'd like to. If
that's the case, let me encourage you to share your
hurt with your husband. But first you may need to
address that pain on your own. Don't try to spiritual-
ize away your grief or pain. Don't deny your problem,
your feelings, or your questions. Go into that tunnel
and feel the pain. In *Honest to God*, Bill Hybels outlines
four steps you can take to move from pain and despair
to hope and genuine joy.

• First, refuse to deny the pain, the frustration, or
the heartache you are experiencing. We are deceitful
and hypocritical when we deny such feelings. We are
not being real when we mindlessly chant, "Praise the
Lord!" in the face of life's harsh realities. Our parents
are imperfect and caused us pain; miscarriages are
times for grief; wayward teenagers tear apart their parents' hearts; unemployment brings feelings of fear and

anxiety; and sexual abuse results in devastation beyond description. This is only a sampling of the heartache that is in this world, and we need to face realities like these. We need to acknowledge our feelings of fear, loneliness, disappointment, and anger.

• Next, honestly tell God how you feel. In the Psalms, David repeatedly—and very openly—speaks of the confusion and pain in his heart: "God, I don't understand this! How can You treat me this way? How can You allow this? Why do the righteous suffer while the wicked prosper? Help me understand this!"

Often, such authentic outpourings of frustration and anger are necessary steps on the path to wholeness and to a genuine faith in God. If we don't ask these questions, we will simply go through the motions of believing in God and never find an inner confidence in His infinite power or His unconditional love. Share your feelings, whatever they are, with your God who is big enough to deal with them and able to help you deal with them, too.

• Discuss your pain, disappointment, or heartache with someone else. Galatians 6:2 tells us to "share each other's troubles and problems, and so obey our Lord's command" (TLB). Relief, comfort, and healing come when we share our inner hurts with someone else. The burden somehow seems lighter. Once-overwhelming issues suddenly become manageable when your husband or a friend shows that he/she understands. Often, sharing brings new insight or the suggestion of a course of action you hadn't thought of. Almost always, sharing means less loneliness in your pain.

• Don't hesitate to seek professional help if your unfinished business is weighty and emotionally debilitating. Hybels writes:

Certainly the healing process requires

divine intervention and spiritual growth. And often loving family and friends can provide the human support and wisdom we need. But there are times when competent Christian counselors can provide the necessary blend of spiritual and psychological perspectives. They can help us uncover and understand significant events in our past. And they can help us resolve tensions and initiate more positive relationships with significant people in our lives.[2]

Acknowledging your real feelings and dealing with them can free you to be the kind of friend Christ wants you to be. Without shedding some cobwebs and first being transparent with ourselves, we'll be limited to a very superficial kind of friendship with anyone else.

Having dealt with your feelings to some degree, make an appointment with your husband. Tell him where you hurt and explain that you truly want to be a friend to him but that your pain makes it hard for you right now. If this kind of interaction is something new in your marriage, the idea of talking so openly to your husband and letting yourself be so vulnerable undoubtedly sounds frightening. Let me assure you that meeting the challenge will result in greater honesty and intimacy in your marriage. Pray about taking this step and seek counsel. When you're ready, know that God will be with you. Know, too, that you are paving the way for a new source of strength for your marriage: genuine and intimate friendship with your husband.

The Rewards of Friendship

You probably don't need to be convinced, but friendship does indeed offer rich rewards. Consider the comments of these people:

Upon the death of his friend A.H. Hallam, the poet Tennyson declared, "'Tis better to have loved and lost than never to have loved at all."

Helen Keller once said, "With the death of every friend I love a part of me has been buried, but their contribution to my being of happiness, strength and understanding remains to sustain me in an altered world."[3]

Jesus taught that we find ourselves when we lose ourselves (Matthew 10:39).

When have you experienced these truths about friendship for yourself? Thank God for those gifts!

The value of friendship extends beyond emotional closeness and connectedness. Research, for instance, shows that lonely people live significantly shorter lives than the general population. In his book *The Friendship Factor*, Alan Loy McGinnis points out other benefits of friendship.

> In research at our clinic, my colleagues and I have discovered that friendship is the springboard to every other love. Friendships spill over onto the other important relationships of life. People with no friends usually have a diminished capacity for sustaining any kind of love. They tend to go through a succession of marriages, be estranged from various family members, and have trouble getting along at work. On the other hand, those who learn how to love their friends tend to make long and fulfilling marriages, get along well with the people at work, and enjoy their children.[4]

Whatever you or your husband's past experiences of friendship, I strongly encourage you to cultivate friendship with your husband, but know that your idea of friendship may differ from his. What do you think of when you think of friendship? Intimate sharing? Talking about feelings and hurts and hopes? In contrast, a man's friendships tend to revolve around activities. A friend is someone who goes fishing, plays tennis, or goes to a baseball game with him. Most of a man's friendships grow out of these associations. Shared activities are the starting point for us men, but let me add that Christian men can take male friendships to a deeper level. We can come to a point of real honesty, transparency, and loyalty that makes a friendship the source of important accountability and encouragement.

Many men in America are seemingly without friends, however. They simply don't have (or should that be "make"?) time for friendships. Whether that's due to the structure of their workday, their personality, or their priorities, the fact is that men without friends experience a real emotional void in their lives. Also, too often men are in competition with each other. For various reasons, we men often experience a degree of distrust and cautiousness around one another. Job titles can also interfere with cultivating a friendship until we come to view one another as God's creation and even as a mission field of sorts. I've learned that, whether men work in a plush office or dig ditches, we are all God's creatures and we all have the same needs. This scriptural perspective has helped me become friends with a variety of men.

The fact seems to stand, though, that women have an easier time with friendships and different experiences of friendship than we men do. Our culture, for instance, permits women to be closer to each other than men can be with one another. Women can hug, cry, hold hands, and interlock their arms as they walk down the street, but men are not as free to do these things.

With this discussion of friendship, we've identified another difference between men and women. Men are activity-oriented and women are relational—and what can you do to bridge that gap? Simply get interested in your husband's activities. That's one way you can be his friend. After all, in the words of another Barnes motto, "You have to be a friend in order to have a friend."

Five Ways to Deepen Your Friendship

For whatever reasons, it's often not as easy for a man to cultivate a friendship as it is for a woman. Furthermore, if your husband doesn't come from a very demonstrative family, he may not have a good male role model for how to be a friend to his male friends or even to you. You may very well have to teach him how to be a friend. And the following five points may help.

1. *Assign top priority to your friendship with your husband*—How important are your friendships? How you spend your time will show you! After all, each of us does what we want to. Nothing gets in the way of our doing what is most important to us. So consider again how important your friendships are to you. Do you say you don't have time for friends—but do you find time to go shopping on a moment's notice? To finish that novel? To catch your favorite television program? If you really want to do something, you'll do it.

And, if you really want to nurture your friendship with your husband, you'll do so. You're right in knowing that it will take time and effort. Friendships don't happen instantaneously, and they don't endure automatically. But the time you invest in your friendship with your husband is time well spent.

Now children do indeed demand time from both

you and your husband, but, as Emilie says, "You were a wife to your husband before you were a mother to your children." Your husband needs to be a priority if your marriage is to be strong and your children secure. After all, one of the best gifts you can give your children is to show them that Mom and Dad are in love with each other and are good friends to one another.

2. *Cultivate transparency in your relationship with your husband*—As we saw at the beginning of this chapter, when we are honest with ourselves about who we are (emotionally and otherwise), we can be a better friend. Our willingness to be open about who we are will encourage trust and openness on the part of another.

So be yourself in your friendships. Be yourself, first of all, to honor God who made you the unique person you are. Take the risk of sharing the joy of your high points and the tears that come at your low points. Also, discover the freedom that comes with being who you are. When our daughter, Jenny, was in high school, she worked in my office. One evening at the dinner table she said, "Dad, you're the same person at work as you are at home"—and I considered that a real compliment. That's the way I want it to be. Besides, life is simpler that way. I'm not smart enough to wear a lot of masks—I couldn't remember which face was for which occasion!

If you dare to take the initiative and reveal to your husband who you are and what you're feeling, your husband is much more likely to reveal his true self. Nothing will be as effective in drawing him out as your transparency.

3. *Dare to risk talking about your affection.* At our seminars, Emilie and I pass out packages of 64 multicolored cards which say, "I love you because . . ." We

encourage our guests to use these little encouragers in their children's lunch pails, their husband's attaché case when he leaves on a business trip, or a letter to a friend. The cards can also be used as place cards on the dining room table when guests come to dinner. We encourage the women to take a few moments to complete the sentence: "I love you because . . . you comb your hair each day; you come to the breakfast table with a smile; you work hard to provide for our family; you are only a phone call away when I need you."

People who have used these cards tell us again and again what a good idea they are, and I'll long remember the woman who put one card in her husband's sandwich. When he unwrapped his sandwich and took a big bite, he discovered the card but thought his wife had left the wrapper on the cheese! Then he realized he had received a special note from his wife. At first he thought his lunchtime buddies would make fun of him, but one of them said, "I wish my wife would send me a love note!" The wife who had written the note was glad she had risked sharing her affection—and I'm sure her husband was, too. We men want to know that you love us!

And there are lots of ways you can show us that you care! Consider what I call "the power of the chocolate chip cookie." When our son, Brad, was about 27 years old and still single, he said that he was looking for a girl who would bake him chocolate chip cookies. Never had one of his steady dates taken the time to bake him cookies. About two years later, when he was dating the woman who would become his wife, Marie showed her awareness of the power of the chocolate chip cookie. When they were dating, Marie showed her love by baking Brad chocolate chip cookies—and she still does so today.

Our dear friends Bill and Carole Thornburg can also teach a lesson about showing love. In 1987 Bill was diagnosed with leukemia. Eighteen months and three rounds of chemotherapy treatment later, Bill went to be with our Lord. Soon afterward, Carole was reading a novel where the main character, who was dying of cancer, left a letter for her husband and another for her young children to read when they became adults. Carole desperately wished that Bill had left her a note.

Several days later, when she was getting ready to visit Bill's brother, she decided to take him some of Bill's old books. While going through the books, she found an envelope addressed to her from Bill. He had written her an Easter card two years earlier, and she had tucked it away in a book. Upon rediscovering the card now, she was so thankful to God for her husband's written words. At Christmastime 1989, Carole had a precious Easter card from her beloved husband. It read:

A Tearful Week
A Long Week
A Hard Week
A Lonely Week
A Painful Week
A Revealing Week
A Recovering Week
A Reassuring Week
A Peace Week
A Rededication Week
A Friendship Week
A Love Week
A Roller Coaster Week
A Renewal Week

A Glorious Week
A Victorious Week
A Life Changing Week
But A Week I Will Never Lose Sight Of

May God be our source of true love and friendship. You have been so good these days. I love you for it. You have been all a husband would desire. Forgive me, Sweet, for not keeping our love fresh. I love you.

Happy Easter and Happy Beginnings,
Bill

Bill and Carole spoke openly of their love for one another, and Bill's words offered Carole a sense of his presence when he was gone. I know something about that, too. I have a picture of Bill and me on my desk, and each morning I say "hello" to my friend. He's still my friend even in death.

4. *Learn the language of love.* Each of us who is married needs to learn how to say, "I love you"—and I'm not talking only about speaking aloud those three powerful words (although that's an important thing to do!). We need to also say, "I love you" through our sensitivity to our spouse, our manners, and our respect. Sometimes, for instance, as Emilie is leaving on errands, she will ask if there's anything she can get for me while she's out. Other times she makes my favorite meal—crispy Southern fried chicken. Or she might hear me say that I'd like a certain new book and—what do you know?—it shows up unexpectedly for no special reason. These are just some of the ways that Emilie shows me that she loves me.

And I show Emilie that I love her with an evening out, a bunch of fresh flowers, a new blouse, and taking out the trash without being asked. However I choose to show my love, I say aloud to Emilie, "Just another way to say, 'I love you!'" Little acts of kindness like this are powerful and effective ways to strengthen your friendship with your mate. Such little acts of thoughtfulness show that you do not take your loved one for granted.

Certain rituals and traditions in our family also enable us to express our love for one another. We kiss each other goodnight and say, "May God bless your sleep." We celebrate our love on anniversaries and birthdays by giving each other small gifts. We telephone one another when we're apart, visit one of two favorite restaurants on special occasions, go out to lunch, attend the theater, and share hugs and (my contribution) corny jokes. All of these things—spontaneous little acts as well as carefully planned events—make for a special friendship.

One word of caution! Be sure that you are expressing your love in the language—the words *and* the actions—that your spouse will understand! Just because you feel loved when he plans a special dinner out doesn't mean that he feels loved when you do the same! Be a student of your husband. Know what best communicates to him the love you have. And keep your eyes open for common, everyday events that give you the chance to express that love!

5. *Give your husband freedom.* As the apostle Paul writes so beautifully in 1 Corinthians 13, "Love is very patient and kind, never jealous or envious, never boastful or proud" (v. 4 TLB). Love is never possessive—and our love for our spouse should not be possessive. A wife's possessiveness too easily becomes demands that control her husband, hold him captive, and suffocate him. Perhaps, for instance, the wife

doesn't give her husband the freedom to fail. Maybe she won't let him forget a mistake he made or a hurt he inflicted despite the command to forgive as we have been forgiven by our heavenly Father (Colossians 3:13). A wife may also discourage her husband and keep him from growing and developing in his spirituality, his work, and even his hobbies. Maybe she won't attend the same church he wants to attend, is rarely—if ever—willing to entertain an important client, or keeps his weekend "honey do" list so long that he has no time for himself.

Men fear losing their freedom, and a wife can easily make that fear a painful reality. But let me say that we men also need to carefully balance our relationship with the Lord, our wife, and our children with our job commitments and recreational activities. We men need to be sure we are making time to be the husband and father God has called us to be. Just as a husband is responsible for letting his wife become all God wants her to be, you wives are to set your husband free to be all that God wants him to be.

How can you set your husband free to become the person God would have him be? Key to setting him free is accepting him unconditionally (unless he is doing something in violation of God's commands). Encourage your husband to be the unique person God created him to be. Be a source of serenity in his life and grant him the solitude he needs to dream, to recover, and to be with the Lord. Encourage him to develop friendships with other men and welcome the new perspectives, interests, and passions these friends may introduce into your husband's life.

Also, be willing to allow for shifts in your husband's friendship with you. As the seasons of your life change, you'll notice variations in your friendship. The birth of a child, for instance, means new responsibilities, increased tiredness, an adjustment in the area of sexuality, and consequently greater demands on your friendship. Your husband can come to feel that the child is more important to you than he is. Then, when your grown children leave home, friendship with your spouse can again be strained. Do the husband and wife still know each other and like each other or, through the years, have they become business partners held together loosely by their child-raising efforts? This "empty nest" time is the real test of a marital relationship and friendship. Whatever the season of your life, know that a friendship that is tended, nurtured, and rooted in the Lord will endure. Know, too, that standing by your man as his friend will also enable your marriage to endure.

Let me close with a poem that offers you yet another way to tell your husband—who is, I hope, your best friend—that you love him.

I Need You

I need you in my times of strength and in my
     weakness;
I need you when you hurt as much as when I
     hurt.
There is no longer the choice as to what we will
     share.
We will either share all of life or be fractured
     persons.
I didn't marry you out of need or to be needed.
We were not driven by instincts or emptiness;
We made a choice to love.
But I think something supernatural happens at
     the point of marriage commitment (or
     maybe it's actually natural).

A husband comes into existence; a wife is born.
He is a whole man before and after, but at a
    point in time he becomes a man who also is
    a husband;
That is—a man who needs his wife.
She is a whole woman before and after.
But from now on she needs him.
She is herself but now also part of a new unit.
Maybe this is what is meant in saying,
"What God hath joined together."
Could it be He really does something special at
    "I do"?
Your despair is mine even if you don't tell me
    about it.
But when you do tell, the sharing is easier for
    me;
And you also can then share from my strength
    in that weakness.[5]

10

Stand by Your Man's Decisions

A friend loves at all times.

Proverbs 17:17

One night, after a meeting at church, several of us got talking about investments, and a friend told me about an airline stock, currently selling for $23 a share, that was expected to sell for $40 a share within 60 days. I was well aware of my friend's great track record when it came to investing, so his information really got my attention. If I purchased a substantial number of shares at $23 a share and then sold them for $40 a share, I could earn quite a profit! Although I had always preached and practiced, "If it sounds too good to be true, it probably is!" I felt that this opportunity was clearly the exception.

The next day I called my stockbroker and told him

to buy the shares. You wouldn't believe what happened to that company over the next few days! One of its planes crashed into the icy waters of Washington, D.C., resulting in the death of many passengers; one of its unions called an all-out strike and shut down the airline; and the chief executive officer left the company and began working for a competitor. And, yes, the stock went down, down, down. When the price hit $13 a share, my friend suggested that I consider buying some more shares to cover my losses and so reduce my price-per-share costs. So again I called my broker and bought more shares, desperately hoping that things would turn around.

I hung onto the stock for another nine months, and the price went down, down, down. At that point, I pridefully decided, "I'm not going to sell it now! It will have to come back up in value." A year later, the company filed bankruptcy and went out of business. My stock was worthless. I had lost thousands of dollars, spent a lot of time on the telephone to both my friend and my stockbroker, and worried a great deal about losing all that money (which really wasn't extra to begin with). Without exception, this venture into the stock market was the worst decision I ever made.

But, despite all the money and time I wasted, Emilie never once reproached me. Not once did she suggest by words or actions that I had failed her. She never once suggested that she thought I was stupid, careless, or not to be trusted with the family money. She stood by me even when I made a series of very poor financial decisions.

Respect

And Emilie was able to stand by me in my mistakes because she had learned—and was able to live out—two wonderful verses of Scripture. In Ephesians

5:33, Paul writes, "Let the wife see to it that she respect her husband," and in 1 Peter 3:4, the apostle Peter writes, "Let [your beauty] be the hidden person of the heart, with the imperishable quality of a gentle and quiet spirit, which is precious in the sight of God."

In obedience to Scripture and out of her love for me, Emilie continued to respect me when I made poor decisions. She also continued to have that "gentle and quiet spirit, which is precious in the sight of God." When a woman possesses this inner peace and tranquillity, she naturally blesses her husband with it. Throughout my financial venture and its aftermath, Emilie's inner tranquillity offered me much peace, and her respect for me never faltered. I was never so thankful for a godly wife as I was then.

I encourage you to respect your husband, too, whatever the circumstances of your life together. You may be thinking, "I'd respect my husband if he ever did anything worthy of respect!" But God doesn't give an out when He issues this command. His Word is very straightforward: "Let the wife see to it that she respect her husband" (Ephesians 5:33). Obey God's command to you. Let the grace of His love enable you to respect your mate and extend to him a tranquil and soothing spirit. This touch of God's grace may change your despair over your husband to hope. As God extends His grace to your husband through you, you may also see your husband doing things worthy of respect as he recognizes that you believe in him and will stand with him.

An Escape from Perfectionism

When you consider whether your husband is worthy of your respect, consider what your standards for him are. Are you expecting him to be perfect? Our culture certainly teaches us to demand perfection and be satisfied with nothing less. No mistakes are allowed here! We want everyone and everything to be perfect!

Furthermore, many of us learned growing up that wrong choices are unacceptable. Teachers demanded the right answers, and parents expected us to comb our hair right, brush our teeth properly, and dress appropriately. We learned that we were "bad" when we made poor decisions, so now, as adults, we may feel practically immobilized when it comes to making a decision. We don't want to be wrong!

Are you, like our society and perhaps like the family you grew up in, demanding perfection from your husband? Are your demands for perfection based on your fantasy about what a man should be? Or are your demands that your husband be perfect connected to your perfectionism for yourself? No one—male or female—can find happiness when they are demanding perfection either in themselves or others. But, notes clinical psychologist Marion Woodman, the modern woman is "addicted to perfection, seized by a drive for power and a need to control and dominate."[1] Many of the women in Woodman's study were high-achieving career women suffering from food disorders. Everything in these women's lives had to be perfect—their body, their clothing, their work, and their man. This quest for a perfect man has led many women from one man to another. Never satisfied, they look somewhere else for the perfect man, whom Toni Grant calls "the Ghostly Lover."[2]

Are you comparing your husband to a Ghostly Lover? A Ghostly Lover results when a woman idealizes her image of a man. Soap operas, for instance, have contributed greatly to the existence of this Ghostly Lover, this "perfect" male. With their portrayal of love, sex, and marriage, these daytime dramas set up artificial standards which few—if any—real-life men can meet. When a wife holds her husband up against this perfect but nonexistent Ghostly Lover, he cannot and will not pass the test. She will notice the blemishes in her very human spouse, and these blemishes can destroy intimacy. It's one thing for young girls to have fantasies about the special man in their future and to grow up with that fairy-tale prince in mind. But mature women let go of that fantasy and come to know an actual man and love him for who he is, not who she wishes he were. After all, it's hard to respect someone who doesn't measure up to your standards— but who can measure up to unrealistic standards based on your fantasies?

It's also hard for many women today to respect their husband because they find in themselves a sufficient degree of security, strength, and competence. If you have achieved that kind of independence from your husband, what can you do? How can you come to respect your husband more? How can you offer him a quiet and gentle spirit? Only through the grace of God and your submission to Him. God alone can help you "not be conformed to this world" and its demands for strong, aggressive, and independent women who don't need or respect men (Romans 12:2). God alone can transform our thinking—men's as well as women's—so that we are not conformed to a world whose message directly conflicts with the Bible's teachings about marriage and relationships.

Demands for perfection—whatever their roots— lead to paralysis, if not also to resentment and a breakdown of love. I can't tell you how important it is that you as a wife give your husband the freedom to fail, to be human, to not be perfect. Your husband needs to find that freedom at home because it doesn't exist anywhere else in his world—not at work, not at church, and not even at his recreation. Let your home be a place where your husband can stop performing and trying to live up to people's standards. Let your home be a place where your husband can simply be himself.

Furthermore, love your husband for exactly who he is. Believe in him and encourage him, but don't hold forth such high and unrealistic expectations that he feels completely inadequate and incapable. How can your man be your hero if he doesn't feel that you believe in him? If you don't give him permission to be who he is? Or if you have unrealistic expectations of him?

A Home as a Trauma Center

A home needs to be a place where your husband—as well as you and the children—can be human and fail without fear of judgment or rejection. A home also needs to be a place of refuge when we experience that judgment and rejection from the world. Our home needs to be a trauma center for our healing.

Not long ago, Emilie and I were in the emergency room of our local hospital. A friend of ours had been in a terrible automobile accident, one so severe that the attending paramedics thought that everyone in the car was dead. After quick use of the "Jaws of Life," they took Jimmy to the hospital. In response to a telephone call from his parents, Emilie and I were soon in the emergency room, too. Right away it was clear that the world of the emergency room is much different from anywhere else. It is a place of fear, pain, screams, tears, and life-and-death decisions. In that room of complicated machines, bright lights, and dedicated doctors and nurses, lives are saved and some are lost.

And that room is a model of what our homes and our churches should be. Family members and friends alike should enter our home, knowing that they are safe and genuinely loved. Sometimes a home may be the scene of pain and screams and tears, but hopefully those things will lead to healing and renewal.

How can you make your home a trauma center for your husband? Start by being sensitive to how he feels when he arrives home. Listen when your husband needs to unload. Give him a few minutes to unwind by himself if he needs it. Try not to hit him right away with the concerns of your day. Let your home be a place of rest and restoration. Then your husband will be better able to give you what you need to find rest and restoration as well.

I also encourage wives—and husbands, too—to spend time with the Lord in prayer. Take time to simply rest in His presence and you'll discover how He can refresh you. A wife who spends time with her Lord will indeed find the refreshment she needs for herself as well as the refreshment, tranquillity, and peace she wants to share with her husband.

Respect Your Man's Abilities and Let Him Lead

A wife shows her respect for her husband when she stands by his decisions, when she is sensitive to what he needs in the home, and when she lets him be the leader in the family. I was reminded how important such leadership is to us men when I was a guest speaker at a men's conference in Southern California a few years ago.

In one of our small Friday evening groups, the men—who were generally reserved and relaxed in their approach to life—started talking about the fact that they were married to opposites, to women they described as verbal, directed, and take-charge people. They wanted to know how they could be leaders in their own homes. These men wanted to lead, but experience had shown them that their mates did not want to follow. These men didn't know what to do, and they were confused about what it meant to be the leader in the home.

As I listened to them talk, I saw that these men—and their wives—did not have a clear understanding about the difference between work responsibilities and home responsibilities. Several of these men were in business with their wives. They saw that their wives were more competent in certain key areas of the business, and, in a few instances, the wife was the president of the company. The wives' strength in the business world caused confusion about the couples' roles at home.

I shared with these men that it isn't unmanly to have your wife be more competent in business, and I cautioned them not to confuse their leadership in business with leadership in the home and the marriage relationship. Wives and husbands need to look at each other's strengths and determine who will perform which tasks at home. I personally feel that whoever is most competent at a given task should be responsible for that task. If, for example, a wife has stronger business and math skills, why not delegate the family banking to her? If a husband is more skilled or more interested in menu planning, shopping, and cooking, he should feel very comfortable contributing those skills to the family. Such arrangements reflect each individual's respect for the other person's abilities.

And I've seen such arrangements work very well. My brother Ken is a gourmet cook who considers cooking his hobby, so he prepares all the family meals. Ken has also been the number one salesperson in his insurance company and elected to its Hall of Fame. Clearly a leader in the business world, Ken is also clearly the leader in his family. His wife, Paula, respects Ken's gifts and so surrenders the kitchen to him. While that may not be the norm, Ken's culinary contributions are one way he uses his strengths to lead. How does the division of labor in your home indicate your awareness of and respect for each other's skills and abilities?

A Look in the Mirror

How your family functions can reveal much about the respect you and your husband have for each other. How you and your husband communicate can also help you take a reading of the level of respect you show one another. A look at two passages will help you look in the mirror.

First, in their book *Choosing to Love*, Jerry and Barbara Cook suggest that wives read the following message to their husbands. Let it be the catalyst for a discussion about your marriage.

> I married a man I respect;
>   I have no need to bow and defer.
> I married a man I adore and admire;
>   I don't need to be handed a list entitled
>   "how to build his ego" or
>   "the male need for admiration."
> Love, worship, loyalty, trust—these are inside me;
>   They motivate my actions.
>   To reduce them to rules destroys my motivation.
> I choose to serve him, to enjoy him.
> We choose to live together and grow together,
>   to stretch our capacities for love
>   even when it hurts and looks like conflict.
> We choose to learn to know each other
>   as real people,
>   as two unique individuals unlike any other two.

Our marriage is a commitment to love;
>   to belong to each other
>   to know and understand
>   to care
>   to share ourselves, our goals,
>   interests, desires, needs.
Out of that commitment the actions follow.
Love defines our behavior
>   and our ways of living together.
And since we fail to meet not only the demands
>   of standards but also the simple requirements
>   of love
We are forced to believe in forgiveness . . . and
>   grace.[3]

Now consider a passage from H. Norman Wright's *Quiet Time for Couples* in which he addresses the issue of respect more specifically. What does this passage show you about your marriage and the respect you show your husband?

> Do you have a respectful marriage? This is part of our calling as believers. Today's passage ["Let each individual among you also love his own wife even as himself; and let the wife see to it that she respect her husband"—Ephesians 5:33] instructs both husbands and wives to respond to one another with respect. But do you understand what that means? Respect in marriage means ministering to your partner through listening, a loving embrace, a flexible mind and attitude, and a gracious spirit. It means looking past faults and differences and seeing strengths and similarities. It means sharing concerns mutually instead of attempting to carry the load yourself.

Consider the following questions as you evaluate your respect for one another:

- In a tense situation, do I cut off my partner when he or she holds a view different from mine?
- When I think my partner is wrong, do I become offensive and harsh trying to put him or her in place?
- In trying to get a point across, am I gently persuasive or opinionated and demanding?
- Am I driven so much by the need to be right that I try to pressure my spouse into my position? Do I intimidate my partner?

Yes, these are questions which meddle. But answering them is a good step toward building a respectful marriage. As one author said, respect begins when we "learn to practice careful listening rather than threatened opposition, honest expression rather than resentment, flexibility rather than rigidity, loving censure rather than harsh coercion, encouragement rather than intimidation."

How's the respect in your marriage relationship?[4]

When we show our mate respect in ways that Norm Wright outlines, we do much to strengthen our marriage. And you, as a wife, have an important opportunity to show your respect for your husband each time he makes a decision, good or bad—and some will be bad. Let me remind you that Babe Ruth struck out more times than any other baseball player—but he also hit 60 home runs in a season and set a new record that no other player has equaled. Keep in mind, too, that today's baseball players make millions of dollars for batting .300—and batting .300 means getting on base 300 times out of 1000 times at bat. Looked at differently, that statistic means *not* getting on base 700 times—and still the world is willing to pay greatly for a performance like that! So perhaps we husbands and wives can be a little more forgiving and respectful when our mates make a few bad decisions. When you can do that for your husband, you will be showing him your love in a very powerful way.

You will also be loving your husband with the love of Christ. "When we fail," Norm Wright observes, "and often we do—God keeps no record of it. God does not deal with us according to our sins (Psalm 103:10), but He accepts us in Christ. Because of the work of Jesus on the cross, you are accepted as blameless. [So] perhaps one of your most important callings in marriage is to follow the model of Christ by being a living benediction to your partner. Help keep your mate from stumbling, and when he or she does fall, don't keep track of it. Scorekeeping isn't a part of marriage; however, forgiveness is."[5]

Stand by your man when he makes decisions. Let go of unrealistic standards of perfection and love him for who he is, a fallible human being. Let your home be a place where he isn't constantly evaluated and where he doesn't have to perform in order to be accepted. Focus on his skills and abilities and let him lead from his strengths. Finally, don't keep track of the poor decisions he makes. Your husband will become a more confident decision maker and a better leader when he knows that you are in his corner no matter what the outcome.

11

Stand by— Through Your Man's Hardness of Heart

Be submissive to your own husbands so that even if any of them are disobedient to the word, they may be won without a word by the behavior of their wives, as they observe your chaste and respectful behavior.

1 Peter 3:1,2

Several months ago, Emilie and I were hosting a radio talk show in Southern California when a lady called in and asked, "How do you love a husband who isn't a Christian?" I thought for a moment and replied, "The same way you would love a husband who *is* a Christian!"

Too often husbands who aren't believers—and even some who are—feel that they are in competition with Jesus for their wife's love. And that is definitely not how to love your husband, whatever his faith! These men often give up on their marriage relationship, realizing that they can't compete for their wife's devotion against someone as good as Jesus. Wives do indeed need to love God with all their heart, soul, and mind (Matthew 22:37), but wives are also to love their husbands even when their husbands have hardened their hearts or strayed away from the Lord.

The Bible's Commands

God's Word offers very specific instructions to wives about how to love their husbands, but many of these passages are hard for twentieth-century believers to accept. Paul teaches us, however, that "all Scripture is inspired by God and profitable for teaching, for reproof, for correction, for training in righteousness; that the man of God may be adequate, equipped for every good work" (2 Timothy 3:16,17). Consequently, we can't ignore those commands which run counter to our culture and our comfort.

And Genesis 3:16 contains two such commands: "Then God said to woman, 'You shall bear children in intense pain and suffering; yet even so, *you shall welcome your husband's affections,* and *he shall be your master*' " (TLB, emphasis mine). These instructions are certainly contrary to what we read in the newspaper, see on television, and watch in first-run movies. These instructions are, however, God's command, which wives choose either to obey or not to obey.

Choosing to obey these commands means choosing to love in the ways that this book has outlined. Specifically, choosing to obey will mean recognizing and meeting your husband's needs, loving him despite the ways he is different from you, and being his friend. It will mean standing by the decisions he makes, good and bad, and standing by him when his heart is hard against the Lord.

Standing by your man when his heart is hard against God isn't easy, but it may be easier if you understand a few things. First, realize that you are not responsible for your husband's salvation. He is. Second, you are not appointed to be the change agent in his life. As I've said before in this book, that's the job of the Holy Spirit. Third, your husband's salvation is a matter between God and him.

So what is your role if your husband's heart is not open to the Lord? Your role is to love him. The Living Bible paraphrases the command of 1 Peter 3:1 this way: "Wives, fit in with your husbands' plans; for then if they refuse to listen when you talk to them about the Lord, they will be won by respectful, pure behavior. Your godly lives will speak to them better than any words." Let those words encourage you to stand by your man—and recognize that fitting in with his plans won't always be easy!

Several years ago at a Southern California women's retreat, one of the 700 women in attendance came up to me after Fred Littauer and I spoke on this very topic. "Bob," she said, "my husband wants us to sell our home and move to a small town at the base of the Sierra Nevada on the way to Lake Tahoe. What should I do?" As she shared more details, I saw that her husband wasn't running away and hiding, that he wanted the best for his family, and that he had thoroughly researched the location before planning to start a new business there, so I said, "Go!" The woman said that she didn't feel at peace about the move, but I still told her to go. After we had talked for 30 minutes or so, she said that she would think about my advice and said goodbye.

A year later at the same conference, this woman came up to me again. She said, "You won't believe what's happened in the last year! I went home and told my husband that I'd move, and since that day he's been a different man. He gained such confidence knowing that I supported the move. We've purchased a lovely home and joined a wonderful church. The children like their schools, the business is doing better than we had expected, and we love it there. Thank you so much for taking the time to share with me your wisdom." She gave me a hug and was on her way through the crowd.

As her story shows, men's hearts do soften when they know their wives respect their decisions.

Thirty-Five Years of Prayer

Emilie and I have a dear friend who has also stood by her husband when his heart was hard against the Lord. Emilie met Ruth at church, but they were both also involved in the Christian Women's Association. Ruth was a very proper and elegant lady and the model of hospitality. When you went to her home for dinner or Sunday brunch, you thought you were at a Ritz-Carlton Hotel. Her speech and body language had the polish of a fine finishing school.

Her husband, George, on the other hand, was a self-made oil executive. He had started out working on the oil rigs of Bakersfield and earned his wealth through good investments. His manners were rough, and his speech was punctuated with four-letter words and God's good name.

Ruth and George seemed to be at opposite ends of the spectrum not just in manners but in their relationship to the Lord as well. Ruth shared that she had prayed every day for George's salvation for 35 years and that he didn't seem any closer to knowing the

Lord than he had on the day they were married. Emilie and I also began to pray for George, and when it became clear that George enjoyed our company, we invited Ruth and him to our home Bible study. When George said yes, we were all startled beyond belief. Ruth and George came faithfully every Wednesday night for a year. During that time, George also started going to church, signed up for the men's retreat, and one Sunday morning accepted Jesus as his personal Savior.

Ruth had faithfully prayed for 35 years that George would come to know the Lord—and God answered her prayers. So how can a wife love a nonbelieving husband? One way is with her prayers. Now there are no guarantees about how or when God will answer your prayers, but perhaps you can find hope in the words of preacher Charles Haddon Spurgeon: "He who counts the stars and calls them by their names is in no danger of forgetting His own children. He knows [you] as thoroughly as if you were the only creature He ever made or the only saint He ever loved." May God enable you to trust in His love and be faithful and persistent as you wait for Him to answer your prayers for your husband.

Reflections in the Mirror

Once again in this discussion of marriage, the issue of respect arises. A hard heart can make respecting your husband as challenging as his bad decisions can. The Bible doesn't offer any escape clauses, though. Paul doesn't list any exceptions in a footnote when he writes the following: "With humility of mind let each of you regard one another as more important than himself" (Philippians 2:3). That is clearly a call to respect!

But respect is a funny thing. When we extend

respect to someone, we often receive respect from that person in return. Perhaps even more importantly, as you respect your husband, chances are that he will begin to grow in self-respect. A person who respects himself will, in turn, undoubtedly call forth more respect from you. It's an exciting cycle to begin, and you play an important role. As Margaret Campolo explains below, you can do much to increase your husband's self-respect:

> Remember how much you enjoyed looking terrible in the funny mirrors at amusement parks when you were a child? It was fun because you knew you really did not look like that. You could always find a real mirror and be sure you were you.
>
> In marriage, each partner becomes the mirror for the other. . . . Often a problem in a bad marriage is that one or both of the mirrors is working like those old amusement park mirrors. A spouse begins to reflect ugly things, and the other one feels that his or her best self isn't there anymore.
>
> Mirrors reflect in simple ways; people are far more complicated. We choose what we reflect, and what we choose has much to do with what the other person becomes. One of the most exciting things about being married is helping your partner become his or her best self by reflecting with love.
>
> Positive reflecting will make your spouse feel good about himself/herself and about you, but it will also change the way you feel. As you look for the positive and overlook the negative, you will become happier about your marriage and the person you married. This will happen

even if your spouse does not change at all! . . .

In a difficult marriage, as in the difficult times of a good marriage, ask God for understanding and the ability to do what is humanly impossible. Jesus is our model. And in reflecting our marriage partners positively, we are following His example.[1]

What about your husband are you reflecting back to him? Are you looking for the positive so that what he sees of himself are his strengths and good points? Do you bring out the best in your husband and enable him to see that when he looks into the mirror of your love? These important questions challenge all of us who are married to look in the mirror at ourselves and determine what kind of mirror we are for our mate.

A Real-Life Example

I will long remember a real-life example of the powerful mirror we can be to one another. Emilie and I were waiting to depart from Ontario Airport when I happened to notice two people. From where I was standing, I could see the back of the woman's head and the smiling face of the man she was with. Their hugs and kisses clearly reflected their love and affection for one another. That man certainly loved that woman!

When it was time for us to board the plane, the two people stepped aside to let us go by. Now I had the chance to see the face of this beloved woman. As we passed by, I quickly glanced her way—and was shocked by what I saw. Hers was not the face of a beautiful lady, as I had expected, but that of an accident victim. Her scars, however, did not keep her man from loving her or from showing the world his love for her! He saw beyond the scars to the person she was inside, and his actions communicated his genuine love for her. I don't know whether or not he was a believer, but he was definitely loving this woman as Christ has loved us—unconditionally (John 15:12).

Perhaps your husband's scars, rather than being on the surface, are hidden in his heart. Can you learn from this couple in the airport? Can you offer him unconditional love despite the hardened heart he bears?

Or can you learn from the wisdom of Billy Graham's wife, Ruth? She says, "Tell your husband the positive and God the negative." Following this guideline may also help you stand by your man with love and respect when his heart is hardened against the Lord and perhaps even against you.

A Son's Love

Often other members of the family play an important role in offering love that can soften the hardest of hearts, and that person's love can be the means by which God does His transforming work.

One afternoon, Emilie called me at my office. A dear friend from San Diego had stopped by the house on his way to a private weekend retreat. He had explained that he needed to get away to seek God's will for his life, and he wanted to talk to me. I said, "Put him on the phone!" When John got on the phone, he asked me to go home so we could talk. Suddenly my plans for the last three hours of the work week changed, and I drove home. I wondered why John so urgently needed to talk.

John met me at the front door, we embraced as we always did, and he said simply, "I don't love Donna anymore, and I think I want a divorce." I was stunned. I had known this godly man for 25 years. We had attended the same church, taught a class for young married couples together, been cabinmates on church retreats, prayed together, laughed together, and cried together. Now this friend was thinking about divorcing his wife. His statement was the beginning of more than two hours of conversation.

During those two hours, we opened our hearts to each other as never before. I learned that John had drifted away from Donna over the past few years and had been emotionally (not physically) attracted to another woman. John told me that he needed this weekend away to decide what to do come Monday morning. Before we left, we prayed together and shed a few tears. My last words to John were the request that he stop back by the house on Sunday to let me know what God showed him.

Early Sunday afternoon John appeared at the door. His face showed a new radiance. I could see that God had lifted John's burden and given him new direction. "What happened to you?" I asked. "You look great!"

Step by step, John told me what had happened from the moment he left our driveway. The setting of his retreat was peaceful, the food was tasty, and some of the men he met were helpful, but the real catalyst for the change he had experienced was a letter from his teenage son. He had discovered the letter when he opened his duffel bag to get his Bible.

The words of John's son were powerful. Part of their power lay in the fact that they were words John himself had shared with his son as his son was growing up. As John put it, "My own son showed me the way and made me realize that I was going to make a stupid mistake." I quote the letter at length because its wisdom can be applied in so many situations.

Dear Dad,

I love you, Dad. You mean a lot to me, probably more than you'll ever know. When I was a child and especially when I was in high school, you were my hero. My relationship with you was and still is one of my biggest sources of pride. I don't know many young men who can boast of a close relationship with their father as I can. But now, Dad, I feel it is my turn to counsel and advise you as you have advised me.

I am convinced, Dad, that the Lord doesn't want you to divorce or separate from Mom. I know this may sound like an easy statement for me to make because I am not suffering as you are, but I am convinced—as a Christian and as your son—that leaving Mom is wrong. Granted, my view is not totally objective, but the Lord and the Holy Spirit have convinced me through prayer and Scripture that separation is not God's will.

I emphatically believe that the answer to your suffering lies not in running away from your problems (which, when you get down to it, is what you're doing) but in renewing your relationship with your Maker, the One who created suffering, who died through suffering, and who is the only One who can conquer suffering. Dad, you know that your relationship with Christ isn't what it should be. You don't study the Word as you should, and you haven't for a long time. You haven't reached out for fellowship, and that has hurt you. You can't do it alone, Dad, and that's what you've tried to do. Your whole Christian faith and indeed much of your life have been based solely on emotion, which is the easiest tool for Satan to use to twist and deceive us.

I really feel that, to find the romantic love you are so desperately searching for, you must reenter a love relationship with Christ, a firm, solid relationship based on Bible study and Christian fellowship. I believe, with all my heart and soul, that once you are completely focused on Jesus, then joy, happiness, and romantic love will fall into place. Psalms 37:5 says, "Commit your way to the Lord, trust also in Him, and He will do it." Now this may take time, and you are by nature impulsive and impatient, much as I am, but the Lord promises great things if you'll just wait. Psalms 37:7 says, "Rest in the Lord and wait patiently for Him." Have patience, Dad. The Lord will provide. Second Corinthians 4:17 says, "For momentary, light affliction is producing for us an eternal weight of glory far beyond all comparison."

Dad, you're kidding yourself if you feel that time will heal the hurt that we, your children, will feel. It won't! Justly or unjustly, we shall always feel rejected and at least partially responsible, especially the three younger ones. And none of us kids deserves the pain we would feel because of your selfishness. Those words may be harsh, but we are involved in a harsh situation. I'm scared for my brother and sisters. Who knows what will happen to them if you and Mom divorce?

I'm also scared for Mom. The other day when you went to Auntie's house, she broke down and cried and told me she hated herself. Do you know how much this hurt me?

It really seems ironic for me to hear you say that you think you love Marcy. Could this be coming from the father who so wisely counseled me in high school not to jump into a relationship, to slow down and evaluate my real feelings? What you are feeling is ego gratification, Dad. How long can that last? How long can pride and vanity sustain a relationship? You're dreaming dreams, Dad, but what is the reality? You're too wise to honestly believe that a lasting relationship can be based solely on attraction—and, honestly, isn't that what you're basing your relationship with Marcy on?

I hope I haven't hurt you with my honesty, but I love you too much not to be honest with you. The Lord loves you and has a plan for you. If you let Him use that plan, He will greatly enhance your life. He can provide answers and He wants to, but you have to let Him. You can read the Word every night, you can reach out for fellowship, and you and Mom can have a Bible study together. (You say you've tried that, but as the leader in the relationship, whose fault is it that it hasn't worked?)

I want to leave you with what Paul says in Romans 8:28—"And we know that God causes all things to work together for good to those who love God, to those who are called according to His purpose." Love the Lord, Dad. Seek openly and honestly His purpose, and all things will work toward good. He has the answers. Don't cop out and don't rationalize. You may struggle and suffer for some time, but the reward He offers for your faithfulness and responsibility will soon bring you such joy and happiness.

I love you, Dad, so, so much. Please heed my words for I believe I have been directed by Christ to say these things.

Love,
John, Your Firstborn

This letter was truly a blessing from God. John and Donna had taught their children God's commandments, and their son's Sunday school teachers and Young Life leaders had built upon that solid foundation. As a result, this letter was used by God in the life of John Sr. Now it hasn't been easy for John and Donna to resolve their differences and rebuild their marriage. But they are committed to their marriage and, with God's help and the prayers and support of family and friends, they are going to make it.

Setting the Stage for God to Work

Consider again that scene from the airport. Think, too, about the letter from a loving son. These are real-life examples of people standing by someone they love. That kind of "standing by" can be tough—but it's not impossible.

Know that, whatever has scarred and hardened your husband's heart, you are called by God to stand by him. Sometimes that standing will mean fervent and faithful prayer. There will be nothing else you can do. At other times it will mean acting out a love and respect you may not feel—and then finding yourself beginning to feel those very things! At still other times, standing by your man may mean biblical and prayerful confrontation by someone who has earned an audience with him. Always, standing by a husband whose heart is hardened will mean calling on God for strength, patience, and hope. Know that He will provide those things. Know, too, that your husband needs you to stand by him. He needs you and your prayers. He needs you to love him for exactly who he is right now, not for who you wish he were. God will enable you to do that. After all, your God is a big God quite capable of performing big miracles, and you are in an ideal spot to witness Him at work in your marriage.

12

Stand by Your Man's Work

Then the Lord God took the man and put him into the garden of Eden to cultivate it and keep it.

Genesis 2:15

Fred Lynn, a nine-time All-Star player for the Boston Red Sox, California Angels, Baltimore Orioles, and Detroit Tigers, knows how closely a man's work and his identity are related. Lynn had a career batting average of .283 with four seasons over .300. He hit more than 20 home runs in nine seasons with a high of 39 and a total of 306. Twice he had 100 or more runs batted in (RBIs) during the season, adding up to a career total of 1,111 RBIs. He won four Golden Glove awards for his defensive play, was the American League's most valuable player as a rookie, and hit the only grand slam home run in All-Star history—and then one day he found himself without a job. The checks of $50,000 to $100,000 he was used to getting twice a month stopped coming in. And his response to the situation was something every man can identify with: "When I was playing baseball I knew who I was, but now that I am no longer playing, I don't know who I am."[1]

I can relate to Fred Lynn, and I'm sure your husband can, too. As mysterious as it may seem to you, we men find a great measure of our identity in our work. Whatever a man's job, it can be a source of either great satisfaction or great dissatisfaction—and often, as a man's work goes, so goes his life.

Created to Work

As the Creation passage teaches, human beings were created in the image of God (Genesis 1:26), and one way we reflect God's image is through our work. Men in particular are made for work, and we must feel a sense of accomplishment and satisfaction in our work or we will not be content with life in general. As many wives have learned from experience, when we men are unhappy in our work, things do not go well at home.

And, sadly, many people—men and women alike—are unhappy in their work. Estimates are that the vast majority of today's working Americans are doing a job that is wrong for them, and my experience in public schools and manufacturing supports this statistic. One reason for this unhappiness is that people's jobs often don't match their temperaments. I owned a manufacturing business when I first learned about temperament differences, and that new understanding helped me see that many of my employees were in the wrong position.

• *Sanguines* need to have fun and be able to talk. If they can't talk or have fun, they'll be restless in their jobs. Sanguines also need to be where their bubbly personality, optimism, sense of humor, and enjoyment of people work for their—and their employer's—advantage. Sanguines also offer employers creativity, the gift of entertaining and cheering up other people, and the ability to ease a tense situation. Sanguines make great receptionists, pastors, sales personnel, tour guides, camp leaders, and speakers.

• *Cholerics* are born leaders who have the ability to take charge of anything, so they need to have a degree of control in their work. With their innate sense of what will work, they can make quick and usually correct judgments. They also accomplish more than other temperament types in a shorter period of time. Cholerics are team captains in high school, and they eventually become presidents of organizations. They thrive in any position that allows them to lead and therefore make great coaches, military officers, job superintendents, company presidents, and police officers.

• Since *Melancholies* need to have things just right, they organize tasks carefully and analyze them thoroughly. Melancholies set long-range goals, establish high performance standards, pay close attention to detail, and follow through on even the tiniest point, making them effective in accounting, cost analysis, computer-related jobs, and long-range planning. Their compassion for the hurting and those in need make Melancholies good doctors, nurses, and dentists.

• *Phlegmatics* want to avoid conflicts and keep the peace at all costs. With their even disposition, pleasing personality, and dry sense of humor, Phlegmatics are well liked. Able to stay calm, cool, and collected, they don't make impulsive decisions. Phlegmatics make good fishermen, truck drivers, counselors, workers, mediators, and social workers.[2]

This knowledge of temperaments helped me look at my employees differently. I could see, for instance, that I had a Choleric in a Phlegmatic's job and vice versa. I had a Melancholy working where a Sanguine would have been stronger. Acting on this new understanding, I rearranged positions within my company. As a result, more employees were content in their work. The individuals benefited—and so did the company.

What is your husband's temperament? Does it match his job? If it doesn't, you may have just discovered a key to greater job satisfaction for him and, with the husband and father more content, a happier home life for everyone.

Two Perspectives on Work

Another key to more satisfaction on the job is understanding God's perspective on work and being able to counter the world's view. In the beginning, the Bible teaches, "the Lord God took the man and put him into the garden of Eden to cultivate it and keep it" (Genesis 2:15). God established work as a holy pursuit, and it should be that for those of us who follow Him today. God has ordained work for the human beings He created, and we are to work—whatever the job or task—for Him. Ultimately, God is our boss. He calls us to work for Him, and He is the One we serve.

Modern American culture has moved far away from this biblical perspective on work. Today, work is rarely considered a holy pursuit or a means of serving God. Instead, work is what we must do to survive. We live for weekends and a reprieve from the time clock and the supervisor. Without goals more noble than earning money to pay the bills, the American work ethic has declined. In their bestseller *Why America Doesn't Work*, Chuck Colson and Jack Eckerd address this decline and show how it is hurting the American family and our future as a nation. As Christians, we have an obligation to take a stand against this declining work ethic and, because we serve the Lord, be the best manager or worker in the company.

And who knows what impact our working for the Lord may have on the company or the office? In 1 Thessalonians 4:1,11,12, the apostle Paul says, "This should be your ambition: to live a quiet life, minding your own business and doing your own work.... As a result, people who are not Christians will trust and respect you, and you will not need to depend on others for enough money to pay your bills" (TLB). According to Scripture, our job performance can be a powerful witness to the people we work with. We may soon find coworkers working for the Lord, too!

Working for the Lord

And what does it mean to do our work as unto the Lord? For one thing, it means redefining the purpose of work. No longer is job satisfaction based on getting what we want. Instead, we evaluate our job according to how much we are pleasing God in our work.

For many years, however, I worked to please my boss. Then one day I began to realize that I had the wrong idea about who my boss was. At the time, I was having a very difficult time trying to please my boss. I didn't seem able to make him happy. I soon realized that he was looking out for himself and using the people around him for his personal gain. The situation was bad and getting worse.

Knowing that things at the office weren't right, Emilie encouraged me to consider making a change.

After much praying, Scripture reading, and talking with friends, we decided it was time to make a move. At the same time, I decided to evaluate who my real boss would be, and God's Word directed my thinking. Ephesians 6:5-10 was especially significant:

> Slaves [employees], obey your masters [employers]; be eager to give them your very best. Serve them as you would Christ. Don't work hard only when your master is watching and then shirk when he isn't looking; work hard and with gladness all the time, as though working for Christ, doing the will of God with all your hearts. Remember, the Lord will pay you for each good thing you do, whether you are slave or free.
>
> And you slave owners must treat your slaves right, just as I have told them to treat you. Don't keep threatening them; remember, you yourselves are slaves to Christ; you have the same Master they do, and he has no favorites.
>
> Last of all I want to remind you that your strength must come from the Lord's mighty power within you (TLB).

This passage and others had much to say to me about how to look at the work I would be doing. Although I would be dealing with an earthly boss, I would ultimately be serving God, trusting Him to guide my work and bless my efforts, and wanting to please Him. Patrick Morley, author of *The Man in the Mirror*, knows what it's like to have this perspective as we work: "When the rush of adrenalin flows through our veins, when our heart quickens from the scent of a deal, when our head pulsates from the thrill of the chase, let's remember the source of such pleasure— work is a holy vocation."[3]

After the Fall

Work is indeed a holy vocation, but it is no longer exactly what God intended it to be. Genesis 3:17-19 tells the story:

> And to Adam, God said, "Because you listened to your wife and ate the fruit when I told you not to, I have placed a curse upon the soil. All your life you will struggle to extract a living from it. It will grow thorns and thistles for you, and you shall eat its grasses. All your life you will sweat to master it, until your dying day. Then you will return to the ground from which you came. For you were made from the ground, and to the ground you will return" (TLB).

The fall—the choice we human beings made to be our own God rather than to obey the Almighty—changed the nature of our work. Note, however, that God curses the soil, not the work. We will indeed struggle all of our lives to make a living from the soil (from our job, our career, our profession), but the means of the struggle—the work itself—is not cursed.

Too often, though, the work itself seems cursed. In Southern California, the freeways take people back and forth to work from 4:30 A.M. until midnight. Some of these people spend two to four hours a day traveling to and from the office, the school, or the factory. They go in early, stay late, work overtime, and drive home to a house they can't afford in the first place—much less landscape, furnish, or enjoy. The husband knows that, if they miss two payments, the house goes into foreclosure, so the wife goes to work. But with this extra income from her job, the working couple adds to the list of possessions they can't afford. They buy boats, recreational vehicles, and all-terrain motorcycles so that on weekends they can escape the home they can't afford. Returning from the desert late Sunday night, they wake up tired early Monday morning and start the same cycle all over again—and that cycle is vicious. The wife can't stop working because of all that her check pays for, and some families even encourage their children to go to work so that they can buy for themselves things they can't really afford and don't really need. This obsession to consume clouds our thinking about what our basic needs are. We let the pursuit of material possessions (the bigger house, the fancier car, the latest fashions, the most extravagant vacation, etc., etc.) interfere with God's calling to us to be a family, and American families are indeed hurting as Moms and Dads pursue a paycheck and leave children home to raise themselves. Such selfishness and materialism are weakening our country. And such selfishness and materialism result, in part, from the fact that too many of us Americans are working for the wrong reasons and the wrong boss.

The Blessing of Work

Despite what our culture says and despite how we ourselves may sometimes feel, the fact is that work is a holy undertaking. As we've seen in Genesis, God intended us who are created in His image to occupy our time with creative and productive efforts that give glory to Him.

> Why would a loving God put His children to work as soon as He created them? Because He knew human labor was a blessing. He knew it would provide them challenges, excitement, adventure, and rewards that nothing else would. He knew that creatures made in His

image needed to devote their time to meaningful tasks.

The writer of Ecclesiastes understood this
when he wrote, "Then I realized that it is good
and proper for a man to eat and drink, and to
find satisfaction in his toilsome labor under the
sun during the few days of life God has given
him—for this is his lot" (Ecclesiastes 5:18). This
writer understood that if we have enough to
eat and drink and if we enjoy our work, we are
blessed people.[4]

Think about when you have felt blessed to have
enough to eat, enough to drink, and the satisfaction of
work you enjoy. Oh, at times the work may be "toilsome." The writer of Ecclesiastes acknowledges that
fact, and your own experience confirms it. At those
times, though, we need to remind ourselves of the
privilege it is to serve God in whatever line of work He
has placed us.

People often ask Emilie and me if we ever get tired
of what we do. We often spend 12 to 16 hours a day at
our work, so we get physically tired *from* the work but
we don't get tired *of* the work. And I see three factors
contributing to this kind of job satisfaction:

- having the right job
- working for the right reason
- seeking the right rewards

Serving the Lord is our reason for work, and seeking to bring Him glory as we serve Him and His people is the reward we work for. And "More Hours in
My Day" does indeed seem to be the right job for us.
Let me explain.

God intends our work to be a natural expression
of who we are. Consequently, people who are most

satisfied in their job are those whose work is consistent with their natural interests, abilities, and talents. They are doing what they like to do and what they're good at. When our job isn't consistent with who we are, we feel out-of-place, insignificant, and either bored or defeated. When our work matches our interests and calls on us to use our God-given talents, we feel as if we are doing something worthwhile, and we can feel challenged without being overwhelmed.

Having the right job, working for the right reason, and seeking the right rewards—how well does your work, inside and outside the home, fit those criteria? And how well does your husband's work fit those criteria for him? Does he have the right job? Is he working for the right reason? Is he seeking the right reward? If your answer to any of those questions is no, you have gained some insight into why your husband may be frustrated with work. Even if you can answer those three questions in the affirmative, your husband will still have days when he feels tired, discouraged, and even overwhelmed. Whatever your husband's work situation, the following suggestions will help you stand by him.

How to Support Your Husband

First, understand how important work is to a man. Your husband undoubtedly feels responsible for providing for his family, and that financial responsibility can indeed be a heavy burden. Aside from that practical aspect, work is important because it gives a man a sense of who he is. We men tend to define who we are by what we do. (In contrast, many women tend to define who they are by relationships, by their roles as wife and mother.) When work goes badly for us, we men may be rightfully concerned about providing for our family, but we will also experience a threat to our ego and identity that our wife may not understand.

Remember the baseball player Fred Lynn? As I said at the beginning of the chapter, I can easily identify with Lynn. Unemployment is extremely hard on a man. When our manufactured-housing plant closed down in the recession of 1982, I was without work for the first time in 26 years—and I was lost. I felt I had no identity. I began helping Emilie with her "More Hours in My Day" seminars (it was something to do until I could get a "real" job), but my understanding of who I was remained at a real low point. Oh, yes, I knew I was a child of God, I knew that He loved me, I knew that He cared about me, and I knew that He would provide for me and for my family. I knew all that, but I kept asking, "Who *am* I?"

One night, when we were doing a seminar in the San Diego area and I was hauling in a load of Emilie's books, tapes, and supplies, a woman met me in the parking lot and wanted to know if I was "Mr. Emilie Barnes." That comment put me two more feet into my grave. I used to introduce Emilie as my wife, and now I am her husband. And for 26 years I had been bringing home the paychecks, and they were all made out to Bob Barnes. Now all the checks were made out to Emilie Barnes. What a change! It took me a long time to get over my feeling of inadequacy.

Fortunately, Emilie offered to me what I encourage you to offer to your husband, whatever his work situation. Emilie remembered and practiced the Four A's— acceptance, adoration, approval, and appreciation— and so was able to encourage me when my identity was threatened by a change in my work. If you, like Emilie, truly understand how important your husband's work is to him, you are well on your way to having a contented mate. You will also be able to encourage him with acceptance, adoration, approval, and appreciation when he hits the rough spots in his work.

Pray for your husband and his work each day. The business climate is brutal, and I can tell you that your husband is continually bombarded with all kinds of temptations. Your prayers can help him stand strong and true to you and to his God. As I've said before, I know that Emilie has prayed for me every day for 37 years. I clearly realize how fortunate and blessed I am to have her stand with me in that way.

Emilie has also stood strong in her faith in God's Word. Together, for instance, we claimed this verse of Scripture, and it strengthened her prayers for me:

> But remember this—the wrong desires that come into your life aren't anything new and different. Many others have faced exactly the same problems before you. And no temptation is irresistible. You can trust God to keep the temptation from becoming so strong that you can't stand up against it, for he has promised this and will do what he says. He will show you how to escape temptation's power so that you can bear up patiently against it (1 Corinthians 10:30 TLB).

There were many times when I knew that Emilie's prayers enabled me to "escape temptation's power." I am so thankful for a wife who prays diligently for me. Perhaps you can follow her example. I suggest, too, that in addition to praying for your husband to stand strong against the temptations that arise in the business world, you may pray for the following:

- His daily walk with the Lord
- The right kind of friends and associates

- His ability to work in harmony with others
- Safety in his travels
- The ability to make good decisions
- The ability to set right priorities
- Contentment in his work
- Continuous work
- Integrity in the workplace
- Your marriage and your children

Be supportive of your husband's work. We men love to have our wives and children interested in what we do, so be enthusiastic about your husband's work. Ask questions and listen to his answers. Read the business section of the newspaper and follow what is going on in his line of work. Keep up with his schedule. Be aware of important clients, meetings, and deadlines. If time, travel, and working conditions permit, visit him at work occasionally and take him out to lunch.

Children also like to see where Dad works and learn about what he does. Besides building a bridge between them and their father, a glimpse into Dad's world can help them learn about themselves. One summer, for instance, our son, Brad, worked at our plant—and he quickly learned that he wanted a college education so that he would have other career options. The motivation to get an education was well worth that summertime experience.

Showing that you are truly interested in your husband's work and getting your children interested in what Dad does can strengthen your marriage and your family. Remember, too, the Bible's teaching that women were created to be helpmates to their husbands (Genesis 2:18) and that they are to fit in with their husband's plans (1 Peter 3:1). Marital disharmony results when husbands and wives disregard these biblical principles. In most successful marriages, the wife readily helps her husband and supports his plans.

Be willing to dream with your husband. Perhaps your husband's dreams are more an irritation to you than a source of shared excitement. Let me offer you a different perspective. Proverbs 29:18 states, "Where there is no vision, the people are unrestrained." In fact, the King James Version says that "where there is no vision, the people will perish." We human beings need to dream. We need a vision to work toward. After all, as the adage says, if you aren't moving forward, you'll slip backward. None of us stays on a plateau for long.

Furthermore, dreams can become goals for the future. I know from my own experience that my dreams for my life—my dreams about the college I would attend, the woman I would marry, the children we would have, the career I would pursue, and the man of God I wanted to become—developed into goals and, with God's blessing, have become realities. The first part of reaching my goals involved dreaming about what my life would be like. So be willing to let your husband dream and share those dreams. Who knows when God will bless a dream and bring greater joy and fulfillment than you can imagine?

Dreams—the dreams your husband and you share for his job, for your marriage, for your children and their future—can help give life direction and motivate you to action. So help your husband dream—and thank God for a husband who has a vision for his job, his marriage, and his family.

Be an encourager for your husband. The apostle Paul calls us to "encourage one another and build each other up" (1 Thessalonians 5:11). The word "encourage" means, literally, "to give courage to another person" and, oh, how we men today need courage! Look around at the worlds of politics, business, and even the church. Men need to have courage to stand up for what they believe to be right, and their wives can help them find that courage. With your prayers, your love, and your unwavering support of him and his work, you give your husband the physical, mental, and moral strength he needs to stand up to whatever pressure he faces.

As H. Norman Wright points out, such encouragement "begins with a heart of love and caring, and it is shared through words, attitudes, and actions. Discouraging words cripple, but encouraging words inspire."[5] So choose with wisdom and care the words you speak to your spouse. Be aware of the power of words—power to do good and to do harm. Words, for instance, that communicate your belief in your husband have the power to do great good. In fact, I believe that your man will never become all he was meant to be until you believe in him and tell him so with sincere words of encouragement. And you can share those words through notes sent to his workplace or in a brief telephone call when you know he's going to have a tough day. Consider how you feel when someone offers you words of encouragement. Now give that gift to your husband.

Being an encourager also means being a cheerleader for your husband. Motivate him, support him, and express your appreciation to him. Also, be willing to run the risk of a job change if he's not happy in what he's doing. I can't say it too often: A man gets a sense of identity from his job. If he doesn't feel significant in his work, he probably won't feel as significant at home. The two go hand-in-hand.

Don't expect to do it all. How can you stand by your husband and his work if you are exhausted by all that you are doing? Although the situation is changing, society's call to us (and perhaps especially to women) to try to have it all and do it all and be everything to everyone is still a loud one. Trying to respond to that call puts tremendous strain and pressure on you and on a relationship. Individually and as a team, wives and husbands have to say no to many opportunities, requests, and demands. Being able to do so releases us from the bondage of conformity and frees up energy for our spouse and our family.

When we lived in Newport Beach, many of our children's classmates and friends had very wealthy parents. As a result, they often came home asking permission to participate in certain activities that just didn't fit in our budget. Our children learned at an early age that we couldn't do it all. Some adults are still trying to learn that lesson.

In fact, although Emilie and I teach seminars on time management, home organization, and how to grow a great marriage, we still struggle with a schedule that gets too full, with priorities that get talked about rather than lived out, with goals that seem unreachable, and with expectations about life that aren't being fulfilled. Being involved in a ministry that demands a lot of time and energy, we aren't able to accept all the invitations we receive, entertain guests in our home as often as we'd like, or go away on mini-vacations for the weekend. We can't do it all—and neither can you. And you'll save yourself a lot of time, money, stress, and frustration by not even trying. Attempts to do it all result in damaged relationships, frazzled children, and discouraged parents and spouses.

Even seventeenth-century preacher John Bunyan knew well the problem of trying to do it all and pursuing goals that weren't worth the effort:

> Behold how eager our little boy
> Is for this butterfly, as if all joy,
> All profits, honors, and lasting pleasures,

Were wrapped up in her—or the richest treasures
    found in her—
When her all is lighter than a feather...
His running through the nettles, thorns and briars
To gratify his boyish fond desires;
His tumbling over molehills to attain
His end, namely his butterfly to gain,
Plainly shows what hazards some men run
To get what will be lost as soon as won.
Men seem, in choice, than children far more wise
Because they run not after butterflies,
When yet, alas, for what are empty toys
They follow them, and act as beardless boys.[7]

What are you and your husband chasing after?
Will it stand the test of time? Will reaching your goal
make any real difference in eternity?

God has called us to enjoy life as a gift, to make the
most of every moment, and to live with reverence
toward God and a keen awareness of the future judgment (Ecclesiastes 2:24, 9:10, 12:13,14). Key to enjoying
the gift of life is having a proper attitude toward work.
At the end of your lives, neither you nor your husband
needs to echo the words of Solomon—"I considered all
activities which my hands had done and the labor
which I had exerted, and behold all was vanity ... and
striving after wind and there was no profit under the
sun" (Ecclesiastes 2:11). Instead, having regarded your
work as the holy pursuit that it is and a higher calling
than most of us imagine, you can end your life waiting
to hear God's, "Well done, my good and faithful servant."

Martin Luther knew the truth about work when he
observed, "A dairyman can milk cows to the glory of
God."[7] I encourage you to stand with your husband,

believing in him and encouraging him as he milks cows, practices law, works on an assembly line, lectures at the local college, or drives a truck—to the glory of God!

13

Stand by Your Man's Masculinity

Be on the alert, stand firm in the faith,
act like men, be strong.

1 Corinthians 16:13

As you women know, despite new social free-doms and technological advances that would make your great-grandmother marvel, your life has somehow not gotten any simpler. Have you ever considered how these changes—specifically the social changes—have affected your husband? A new way of life for the American male has definitely emerged since the eighties.

Little more than a generation ago, life was far simpler for the American male. More often than not, he was family patriarch and bread-winner. His wife catered to his needs and raised his children. His word around the home was law.

Not any more. As a result of the women's revolution and economic pressures, men today face a world in which macho is no longer enough. The new and improved model of male is expected to share in breadwinning and child-rearing and be both tender and tough. Where once independence and aloofness was desirable, now openness, sensitivity, and intimacy are prized....

Many [men] struggle to blend vestiges of traditional masculinity with what are regarded as softer, or feminine, traits. "Men are confused and searching for their identity," says Mathilda Canter, a psychologist in Phoenix.[1]

In our confusion that arises from the mixed messages we receive from our culture, many of us men bounce back and forth from being tough to being tender. What does it mean to be a man today? As a wife, you can play an important role in shaping your man's image of himself, and you do this by supporting his efforts to be a man of God.

In 1 Corinthians, the apostle Paul says, "Be on your guard; stand firm in the faith; be men of courage; be strong. Do everything in love" (16:13,14 NIV). He exhorts men to be men and to act like men. Paul calls us men to develop and maintain a vital relationship with God so that we can successfully follow the four important guidelines he sets forth for believers. These commands are for men and women alike, but I'll apply them here specifically to us men.

• "Be on the alert." We men need to be aware of the power of Satan and the temptations he introduces into our life. Then we will be able to call on God to help us stand strong and be the people He calls us to be.

• "Stand firm in the faith." Our faith in the Lord— our devotion to Him and our commitment to serve Him—is to be the source of our strength. Our culture may perceive such faith as foolishness and weakness, but we who believe know that "the foolishness of God is wiser than men, and the weakness of God is stronger than men" (1 Corinthians 1:25).

• "Be strong." Again, we men need the support of our wife as well as the power of the Lord to enable us to stand strong in what we know is right. The demands of the business world can pressure men to compromise their morals. The raising of children calls for integrity, too, as well as a godly strength that gives us patience, wisdom, and love for that important task.

• "Do everything in love." When we men act in love, we can lead with strength and sensitivity, toughness and tenderness in the family as well as in the business world. When we submit ourselves first to Christ out of love for Him, we men find real power. We don't worry about being macho. Instead, we find ourselves being the men God created us to be.

As a woman and a wife, you can do much to bring out these virtues in your man. By standing with him and supporting his walk of faith, you encourage your husband to pursue the path God calls him to. You are not to be at war with him. Instead, be a student of him. Learn what he needs and how you can be most supportive. Recognize, for instance, that a man will go to great lengths to mask or disguise his true self until he can trust the woman of his life. Our lack of commitment to a woman is just one way we build a wall of protection around ourselves—we don't want to be rejected! You can counter this male tendency and ease this male fear by showing yourself trustworthy and clearly expressing your love and support.

Let me also remind you that, despite our defense mechanisms, we men need love, compassion, and kindness. Sometimes we need that love to be communicated through sex and at other times through spiritual guidance. Sometimes we need mothering, and other times we need a cheerleader. Because your husband's needs are best met in different ways at different times, you must become a student of your husband. Get to know him as well as you know yourself. Does this sound like a lot of work? Let me share another Barnes motto: "Successful people do what unsuccessful people aren't willing to do."

I would add here that God will support you in your efforts to know and support the husband He has given you. The writer of Proverbs says this: "By wisdom a house is built, and by understanding it is established; and by knowledge the rooms are filled with all precious and pleasant riches" (24:3,4). Ask God to give you wisdom, understanding, and knowledge when dealing with your husband and building your marriage, and know that the rewards and blessings are abundant. Let me offer you the following insights to help you on your way.

Make Your Husband a Better Man Than You Are

The social changes I mentioned at the beginning of the chapter have given women new freedom, independence, and power, traits long considered more masculine than feminine. With this new territory have come other traditionally masculine traits like assertiveness, aggressiveness, toughness, and dominance. Many women today are too masculine in their approach to life, and their behavior certainly doesn't help a man understand his role as a man.

I suggest here that you consider the truth of the old adage "Opposites attract." In light of this age-old wisdom, I propose that one way you can help your husband stand strong in his masculinity is to be firm in your femininity. And being comfortable in your femininity comes more easily when a man is comfortable in his masculinity. Consider what Toni Grant has observed about these male-female dynamics in her definitions of a "Good Man" and a "better man":

A Good Man is dependable, committed, considerate, loyal, hard-working, protective, and respected by other men in his field. Most of all he has courage and integrity. . . . A woman does not choose a Good Man—her hero—in quite the same way as she would choose a good lover or playmate. A Good Man, in fact, often does not make a good playmate, and may even at times seem—well—just a little bit boring. Yet this tendency toward predictability is a key sign that the gentleman in question may indeed be a Good Man, a man a woman can count on, a better man than she is.

A better man, quite simply, is a man who has strengths and attributes which the woman can admire and respect, attributes which in some way allow her to yield a certain amount of personal control to him, for she knows that this man—the man she is to view as her hero—is trustworthy and dependable. Without this trust in him, it is impossible to relinquish any control whatsoever, and the woman continues to function in the male role. When with a man she can trust, however, the woman is then able to relax into her femininity, cheerfully relinquish some of her control, and enjoy some of the pleasures of being woman. In short, then, a man who is a hero is a trustworthy man to whom a woman feels she can safely surrender and with whom she feels some sense of personal completion.[2]

When you let your husband become a hero to you—when you respect him (Ephesians 5:22,23) and support him—you will see him stand strong in his masculinity. If your husband cannot be a hero to you, then you will either find a different hero or become your own hero. Either option will cause distance between you and your husband and weaken your marriage.

When your husband is your hero, however, he will bring out your femininity. As she alluded to earlier, Grant observes,

> Women are best able to live out their feminine aspects when they give over some of their male dominance to the opposite sex freely and unconditionally. When a woman is willing to do this, she inspires enormous confidence in her man and enhances not only his masculinity but her own femininity as well."[3]

Women who are comfortable with their femininity are able to stand by their man's masculinity. These women also use their femininity to magnetize and encourage their man. They don't—as many women today do—play the traditional male game of "The Quest." They don't run after a man, manipulate the situation, capture him, and then leave when they find themselves no longer interested in him. Instead, a woman who is comfortable being feminine, will draw a man to her like a magnet attracts iron filings. In marriage, too, your femininity can draw your husband to you. Your confidence, your security in who you are as a woman and a child of God, and your feminine mystique will serve as a magnet. So develop that mystery, don't be predictable, and allow your husband to pursue you. If you keep your husband guessing, he'll find himself thinking about you, missing you, and wanting to be with you. Also, keep learning more about how to use your feminine ways to engage and excite your husband. Change your hair, try a new perfume, or kidnap him for the weekend. You'll enrich your husband's life and free him to be more masculine.

Practice Mutual Submission

As his wife, you stand by your man's masculinity by being feminine and, second, by being submissive to him just as, out of reverence to Christ, he is submissive to you (Ephesians 5:21). When we are submissive to one another, we are free to serve and help each other out of love. And your freely given service and love will help your man be strong in who he is as your husband, as a father, and as a provider—and I know that from my own experience.

Recently in Louisville, Kentucky, a woman had watched me assist and encourage Emilie during the conference and commented that I had been a real witness to her. I had indeed submitted to Emilie in terms of the roles we played that weekend, but the thought crossed my mind that in a different situation the roles could have been exactly reversed. After all, Emilie and I are not in competition with one another. In our marriage, Emilie and I have discovered the truth of the Chinese proverb that says, "In submission there is strength." We do indeed find strength when we submit one to another—when we honor and serve each other in every aspect of our life and try to complement each other. Furthermore, we easily submit to one another because, ultimately, we both live in submission to Jesus Christ (again, Ephesians 5:21).

Remember that one way to show your love for your husband is by communicating to him your complete acceptance of him. Serving him in love is one way of expressing such acceptance. Remember, too, that we men clearly recognize the difference between being accepted and merely being tolerated! There may be certain things about your husband that you would like to change, but you are not to be the agent of change in his life. Men change—but only when they are motivated to do so. Perhaps rather paradoxically, change comes when we feel accepted just as we are. And, again, you indicate your acceptance and strengthen his confidence in his masculinity when you submit to him.

Consider the following picture of a relationship:

I love you not only for what you are,
But for what I am when I am with you.
I love you not only for what you have
        made of yourself,
But for what you are making of me.
I love you because you are helping me to make
Of the lumber of my life
Not a tavern, but a temple;
Out of the words of my every day
Not a reproach, but a song.
I love you for the part of me that you bring out;
I love you for putting your hand into
        my heaped-up heart
And passing over all the foolish, weak things
That you can't help dimly seeing there,
And for drawing out all the beautiful belongings
That no one else had looked quite far enough
        to find.[4]

How closely does this poem reflect your marriage? How would mutual submission rooted in a committed love for God help bring about this kind of marital relationship? Mutual submission frees a husband and wife to be the people God calls them to be. It helps you and your spouse, like artists, bring "to the canvas of each other's life the potential that God placed there."[5]

Support Him When He's Low

Do you remember Black Monday, October 19, 1987? On that day, the stock market took a sudden and severe nosedive, falling so fast that many sellers could not get out of the market in time to save their investments. Many investors lost thousands of dollars, and some lost millions.

One man lost $250,000. How would you react if you watched a quarter of a million dollars disappear before your very eyes? How might your husband react? Would you or he jump off a bridge or turn to alcohol to ease the pain? This man did neither because he had learned that his home was a trauma center. He phoned his wife, calmly told her what had happened, and asked her to join him for dinner. They went out to dinner and discussed the day's happenings just as they had done many times before when far less shattering events had occurred.[6] This wife knew how to stand by her man, and her man clearly knew that she was there for him even at a low point when he was undoubtedly feeling very inadequate in his male role as provider for the family. He knew that his wife would accept him.

In *Women and Sometimes Men*, Florida Scott-Maxwell points out that you women often see your husband's low points and "lesser side."

One of the poignant paradoxes in the life of a woman is that when a man comes to her, he so often comes to recover his simple humanity and to rest from being at his best. So a woman frequently has to forego his better side, taking it frequently on trust as a matter of hearsay, and she accepts his lesser side as her usual experience of him. . . . She longs to see his greatness but has to meet the claim of his smallness.[7]

Be available to your husband when he comes to you tired, angry, hurt, and moody. Give him the mothering he needs at those times. Trust that his "better side" will again shine through, but in the meantime, follow the example of this investor's wise wife. She had learned to support her husband when he needed her. Even in the face of tremendous loss, she knew how to preserve her husband's dignity and keep him from being overwhelmed by a sense of inadequacy. As a student of her man, she was sensitive to his needs—and you can be, too. Use that mysterious intuition God has given you to determine what your husband needs. Remember how you have helped him feel supported in earlier hard times and offer him the same kind of love now. And be sure to pray for your husband when he is struggling.

Also, don't be afraid to share tears or, at the other end of the spectrum, laughter with your husband when he's down. Your tears—heartfelt, not phony—may communicate your compassion and love better than any words could. Your tears may also bring out the protectionist and strongly masculine part of your man, and you may see him rise above the circumstances or pain he is dealing with.

At other times, a lighter touch may be appropriate. When we—men as well as women—start taking life or ourselves too seriously, we need an opportunity to laugh. In fact, one of the qualities I like most about

Emilie is her ability to laugh, and she has a wonderful laugh. Our friends, neighbors, children, and grandchildren know Emilie's laugh, and they know that she is fun to be around. Use the gift of laughter carefully and it will serve you well.

Accepting your husband when he is most needy—whether with sympathetic silence, tears of compassion, or the light touch of some humor—will help him, and your marriage, weather the storms of life.

Build Up Your Husband in the Eyes of Your Children

As a man, I can tell you that nothing gives me a sense of my masculinity like being a father to my children—and Emilie did much to help me become a better dad than I would have been on my own. While you are not responsible for developing a good relationship between your husband and your children, you can help him become a better father. Here are a few suggestions.

• *Give Dad a chance to learn to be a good father.* Much about the role of a father has changed dramatically since our grandfathers' era. We men now go to childbirth classes and into the delivery room. We carry our newborns, feed them, change their diapers, and, in general, find ourselves very much involved in our children's life. I encourage you, as a mother, to let this happen in your home.

Despite these positive changes, too many women don't give Dad a chance to do more. These moms don't leave the children alone with Dad. Maybe it's because his way with the child, his more relaxed approach to a schedule, or even his diapering technique is different from Mom's. The fact is that children need the opportunity to build a relationship with him apart from you, whatever his diapering or cooking skills! So get involved in church activities or take a class. Give your children and your husband the chance to be together whether for an evening, a weekend camping trip, a day-long fishing expedition, an afternoon hike, or a round of golf. Your husband will feel more competent as a father—and therefore more sure of his masculinity—when he feels confident about his relationship with the children.

• *Let Dad become his own kind of father.* Dad needs to be free to do things with the kids that you, as their mother, won't do. Your choices of activities with the children may be safer, neater, and cleaner than Dad's choices—and that is okay. But your children also need to share Dad's kind of fun with him, and that may mean hunting, surfing, skiing, woodworking, or tinkering with the car. At times there will be scratches, torn clothes, stained T-shirts, and smashed fingers, but children will be building a relationship with Dad and seeing him model what being a man is all about.

Gordon Dalbey challenges fathers to call their boys out from their mother so that their sons can become men. Dalbey states, "If a boy's manhood has never been confirmed by identifying with the larger community of men through his father, he constantly seeks it with woman after woman, remaining forever `invalid' in his manhood."[8] It is vital that children—daughters as well as sons—get to know their fathers at play, at work, in church, in all aspects of life. Such interaction also builds up Dad!

• *Make Dad your hero and he'll be your children's hero.* You've probably heard it said that it's not so much what our children are taught that counts, but what is caught. One important lesson that can be caught by your children is that Dad is a hero, and they'll catch that lesson when they see that he is your hero.

When I was a high school student, I caught my dad hugging and kissing my mom at the kitchen sink each evening as she washed the dishes and he dried them. While they cleaned up after dinner, they talked about the day's activities, and in the process Dad sent little "love tokens" to Mom. While the hugs and kisses were primarily for the two of them, those love tokens also showed us boys that Dad loved Mom—and what a gift of security that was to us. So when I grew up and started a family, I offered the same love tokens to Emilie, and our children caught us in the act. And— you guessed it—today our grown children are sharing love tokens with their spouse in their kitchen.

Children notice how their parents treat each other, and your children will be well aware of how you treat their father. It is therefore critical that your words and actions are consistent with one another. If you say you love your man but your actions suggest otherwise, your children will not hear your words. When your actions do consistently reflect the love you say you have for your husband, you will be nurturing your children's relationship with their father. When your words *and* your actions indicate your love and respect for Dad, you kids will catch it and learn to love and respect their father.

Emilie always did a great job making me a hero to our children. As my biggest fan, she always spoke positively about me even when I wasn't around. I don't remember her ever criticizing me or being anything but completely supportive in front of the kids. (Oh, we had our differences, but we discussed those in private rather than in front of the children.) And there are many ways to express your support and love for Dad in front of the kids. Compliment his new shirt. Notice his great haircut. Say, "Thank you" when he does something for you. Comment on his ability as a golfer or tennis player. Tell him how much you appreciate the fact that he is a good provider. Acknowledge the long drive he makes on the freeway in order to go to work. Let him know that you value his role as husband and father. In short, make Dad the hero. Let your children clearly see that you love and respect their father.

When you do this, Dad—as well as the children—realizes that he is significant to the family. You remind him that who he is to you and the children and what he does for the family are very important. And Dad's masculinity receives the strengthening it needs.

I remember all too clearly a time when I needed that kind of nurturing. I had had a very stressful day and wasn't feeling good about myself. Handing the paycheck over to Emilie, I said, "I think the only reason I exist is to provide a check for this family!" Although caught off guard by that statement, Emilie was sensitive enough to see that I was struggling with my identity. It wasn't long before she and the children were expressing appreciation for Dad. They were no longer taking for granted the paycheck or the provider, and I greatly appreciated their reminders that I was important to them.

Your husband is probably a lot like me, so let him know that he is important to you. Be a model for your children so that they can also tell Dad that they love him and appreciate him. As your husband sees himself reflected in the mirror of your love, he will become a stronger leader, more devoted father, and more loving husband. With this kind of encouragement, you will do much to strengthen your husband's identity so that he will have the confidence he needs to be a man of God at home and at work.

Strong and Sensitive

Let me close this discussion of your husband's masculinity with a striking model of a man who was both strong and sensitive, tough and tender. Although this man—a Civil War soldier—lived a hundred years ago, he can teach husbands and wives much about committed love and a masculinity that is strengthened by a wife's devotion and, in turn, gives her strength. Major Sullivan Ballou wrote this letter to his wife a week before Manassar, the first Battle of Bull Run.

July 14, 1861
Camp Clerk, Washington, D.C.

My very dear Sarah,

The indications are very strong that we shall move in a few days—perhaps tomorrow. Lest I should not be able to write again, I feel impelled to write a few lines that may fall under your eye when I shall be no more . . .

I have no misgivings about, or lack of confidence in, the cause in which I am engaged, and my courage does not halt or falter. I know how strongly American Civilization now leans on the triumph of the Government, and how great a debt we owe to those who went before us through the blood and sufferings of the Revolution. And I am willing—perfectly willing—to lay down all my joys in this life, to help maintain this Government, and to pay that debt.

Sarah, my love for you is deathless; it seems to bind me with mighty cables that nothing but Omnipotence could break; and yet my love of Country comes over me like a strong wind and bears me unresistibly on with all these chains to the battlefield.

The memories of the blissful moments I have spent with you come creeping over me, and I feel most gratified to God and to you that I have enjoyed them so long. And hard it is for me to give them up and burn to ashes the hopes of future years, when, God willing, we might still have lived and loved together, and seen our sons grow up to honorable manhood, around us. I have, I know, but few and small claims upon Divine Providence, but something whispers to me—perhaps it is the wafted prayer of my little Edgar, that I shall return to my loved ones unharmed. If I do not, my dear Sarah, never forget how much I love you, and when my last breath escapes me on the battlefield, it will whisper your name. Forgive my many faults, and the many pains I have caused you. How thoughtless and foolish I have often times been! How gladly would I wash out with my tears every little spot upon your happiness . . .

But, O Sarah! if the dead can come back to this earth and flit unseen around those they loved, I shall always be near you; in the gladdest days and in the darkest nights . . . *always, always,* and if there be a soft breeze upon your cheek, it shall be my breath, as the cool air fans your throbbing temple, it shall be my spirit passing by. Sarah, do not mourn me dead; think I am gone and wait for thee, for we shall meet again.[9]

Sullivan Ballou was killed at the first battle of Bull Run, but he had left his wife these few lines of love. She undoubtedly read her beloved husband's words and thought of him whenever a soft breeze touched her cheek. Her husband had been both strong and sensitive, both tough and tender. As his letter reflects, he faced death with courage, standing strong in his convictions and unwavering in his commitment to his country, his wife, and his God. And I would guess that some of his courage resulted from a wife who believed in him, encouraged him, and made him her hero. Sarah had undoubtedly stood by her man's masculinity.

Supporting your man's masculinity will indeed encourage him to be the man—and husband and father—that God wants him to be. Like Sullivan Ballou, who was both tough and tender, your husband can come to know the strength of his masculinity. He can know the balance between strong and sensitive that God intended when He made man. I'm sure God looked down upon Major Ballou and said, "It was good." You can help your man earn those same words of praise.

14

Stand by Your Man: Some Concluding Thoughts

The husband is the head of the wife,
as Christ also is the head of the church,
He Himself being the Savior of the body.
But as the church is subject to Christ,
so also the wives ought to be to
their husbands in everything.
Husbands, love your wives,
just as Christ also loved the church
and gave Himself up for her.
Ephesians 5:23-25

As I close this book, I am reminded of something my dear friend Bill Thornburg said when he faced his third bout with cancer and chemotherapy was no longer a possibility. His doctor told him, "Bill, go home and have a wonderful

August, and I'll see you again in September." At the same time that Bill shared his doctor's words with me, he told me he was going to write a book called *My Shrinking World*. Together, the doctor's words and the title of Bill's book have a message for all of us.

Not one of us knows if we're living through August, and none of us knows whether we'll see September. And few of us are aware of how our world may be shrinking. We don't know how much time we have, so we need to cherish each day God gives us with our spouse and our children. So I challenge you to enjoy the time you have with your husband and your children.

My prayer for you is that your August will indeed blossom into a wonderful September and into many other wonderful months. My prayer for you is that your world, which may seem to be shrinking and crowding in around you—will open up so that you can clearly see God's perfect will for your life and experience His will for your marriage. That's why I wrote this book.

How Will You Respond?

Stand by your man! That has been the rallying cry of this book, and it's a cry that needs to be shouted throughout our land and acted on by wives from Hawaii to New York, from Alaska to Florida. Society needs families that stay together, children need happily married parents, and husbands need wives who are committed to them. Will you respond to the call to stand by your husband?

Now I am well aware that some women cannot stand by their man because of immoral and/or abusive behaviors. (If you are in such a situation, you must remove yourself and your children from it for your own safety and the safety of your children.) But this book has not addressed those tragic situations. Instead, I have been speaking to women who are discouraged, impatient, confused, or disappointed. And if those words describe you, I say, "Don't throw away a diamond in the rough." I challenge you to stand by your man and work to make your marriage the kind of relationship that God designed marriage to be, a relationship that reflects Christ's love for the church and the church's devotion to her Savior.

As a spokesperson for your husband in these pages, I hope that you have come to understand more clearly the pressures, the challenges, and the needs of your man. Now let me take one final risk and put into your husband's mouth the following words—words which he may want to speak but, for whatever reasons, may be unable to share with you right now.

My dearest wife...

Thank you for choosing me to share your life with you. Thank you for your honesty and transparency. I know it can be painful at times.

Deep down inside I really know that you love me. But I'm a man and I need tangible reminders of your love. There is very little in this life of greater value to me than your love. I need it. I need you.

Could I ask a favor? I love to receive letters from you, but I don't ever want to ask for them—it takes the fun out of receiving them if it's my idea. But would you write me a letter?

I need to know:
- how you appreciate me...
- what I've done to show that I respect you...
- how I've been an encouragement to you...

- that you appreciate the "little things" I do every week for you...
- of your unconditional acceptance, just as I am (Is it there? I need to know)...
- how I am a partner to you...
- why you enjoy me...
- what you like about me...
- how I've changed for good or ways that you've seen me grow (I forget sometimes)...
- that you want to meet my needs...and
- that your love will persevere.

You can write it any way you'd like, but please tell me. I really do love you.

I love you,
Your husband

P.S. I'm not perfect either, but I'm glad we're in this thing together.[1]

What do you think of this letter? How would you respond if you had in fact received it from your husband? What would you write back in response? I invite you to write that letter—and then I challenge you to give it to him!

Be a Risk Taker

I know that meeting that challenge calls you to take the risk of being open, honest, and transparent, and that may mean taking the risk of being laughed at, ignored, or rejected. Even within a marriage, taking this kind of risk may be very threatening, but taking that risk is better than the alternative of shriveling up and dying as a couple. Perhaps the following thoughts will encourage you to take the risk of finding new intimacy and therefore new joy and delight in your marriage:

To laugh is to appear the fool.

To weep is to risk appearing sentimental.

To reach out for another is to risk involvement.

To expose feelings is to risk exposing your true self.

To place your ideas, your dreams, before the crowd is to risk their loss.

To love is to risk not being loved in return.

To live is to risk dying.

To hope is to risk despair.

To try is to risk failure.

But risks must be taken because the greatest hazard in life is to risk nothing.

The person who risks nothing does nothing, has nothing, and is nothing.

He may avoid suffering and sorrow.

But he simply cannot learn, feel, change, grow, love, and live.

Chained by his certitudes, he is a slave.

He has forfeited freedom.

Only a person who risks is free![2]

Take the risk of standing by your man—and of standing close to him. You really do have much to gain!

Stand by Your Man

Just as some aspects of marriage probably never change, some advice for marriage probably never changes either. Such seems true for the following ideas which date back to 1951—and probably long before then! As you read this counsel (some of it may seem a little dated, but some of it is timeless), listen for what God would have you apply to your marriage:

—Show [your husband] in a thousand little ways

that you love him and think he's a wonderful person. Romance dies through indifference and neglect. You can keep it alive by being a responsive lover, by looking attractive, and by using some of the feminine ways that God has given you.

—Remember that a man also needs appreciation and flattery. If he gets it from his wife, he's far less likely to look for it elsewhere.

—Make your husband feel you're the one person in the world whom he can always rely on for sympathy and understanding. Earn his confidence by keeping his secrets. Rejoice in his triumphs and sympathize with his defeats. Don't belittle his accomplishments or laugh at his mistakes.

—Interest yourself in things that interest him so you can enjoy them together. When you share many interests, you get keener pleasures from each other's company and have endless topics for conversation.

—This means taking care of your share of the domestic load. It means keeping the home clean and attractive, being a good cook and a thrifty shopper. It means being cheerful even when times are hard and encouraging him when he is losing faith in himself. It means doing all you can do to help him get ahead by discussing his business problems with him and making friends for him.

—Keep you husband amused and entertained, and be ready to go out on the town when he's in the mood. Many men seek outside recreation alone because their wife is too busy with household details or other interests, or because she is too dull to provide an evening's diversion. Other men go out alone because their mates are killjoys or worrywarts.

—The impression people get of your man will

depend largely on what you say about him, and how you act toward him in public. Don't play the martyr or look for sympathy at the expense of your husband. As you make only favorable remarks about him and act as if he's a fine person, you'll be helping him as well as yourself.

—No matter how old your husband is, he still needs to be babied and cuddled once in a while. He needs to be watched and worried over when he's ill.[3]

Do some of those ideas sound familiar even though they were first broadcast over 40 years ago? Do they remind you that you are not alone in the challenges you face being a wife? Do they encourage you to reach out to your man—whatever the risk?

The Battle Cry

As I've said throughout the book, I say again—stand by your man! And you can do this when you stand by your God and by your commitment to Him and the commitment to your husband that you made before Him. Be sensitive to and willing to meet your man's needs. Understand how he is different from you and realize that different doesn't mean superior or inferior. Be your husband's best friend. Stand with him when his decisions don't work out and when his heart is hard toward God and even toward you. Support his work and encourage him to be confident and strong in this society which is confused about masculinity.

Yes, it's a tall order, but I'm sure that no one ever told you that marriage would be easy. As I wrote at the beginning of this book, know that in the strength of the Lord and with the guidance of His Word, you can indeed meet the challenges and stand by your man even when you feel like quitting!

Notes

Chapter One

1. These ten lies are quoted from and the discussion of them based on pp. 3-10 from Dr. Toni Grant's *Being a Woman* (New York: Random House, 1988).
2. "Barbara Bush Chided at Wellesley College," *Los Angeles Times*, June 2, 1990.
3. "The Best Advice I Ever Heard," *Press Enterprise*, May 12, 1991.

Chapter Two

1. Sherwood Elliot Wirt and Kertsen Beckstrom, *Topical Encyclopedia of Living Quotations* (Minneapolis, MN: Bethany House Publishers, 1982), p. 215.
2. Larry Crabb, *The Marriage Builder* (Grand Rapids, MI: Zondervan, 1982), pp. 105-106.
3. Dennis and Barbara Rainey, *Building Your Mate's Self-Esteem* (San Bernardino, CA: Here's Life Publishers, 1986), pp. 74-75.
4. Bill Hybels, *Honest to God* (Grand Rapids, MI: Zondervan, 1990), pp. 53-54.

Chapter Three

1. Based on Emilie Barnes' *Things Happen When Women Care* (Eugene, OR: Harvest House, 1990), pp. 16-24.
2. Ibid.
3. June Hunt, *Seeing Yourself through God's Eyes* (Grand Rapids, MI: Zondervan, 1989), p. 33.
4. H. Norman Wright, *Quiet Times for Couples* (Eugene, OR: Harvest House, 1990), p. 35.

Chapter Four

1. Robert Fulghum, *All I Really Need to Know I Learned in Kindergarten* (New York: Ballantine Books, 1986), pp. 29-31.
2. Ibid., p. 31.
3. H. Norman Wright, *Making Peace with Your Partner* (Waco, TX: Word Books, 1988), adapted from pp. 173-174.

4. Mordecai L. Brill, Marlene Halpin, and William H. Genné, eds., *Writing Your Own Wedding* (Chicago: Follett, 1979), pp. 88.

Chapter Five
1. Toni Grant, *Being a Woman* (New York: Random House, 1988), p. 55.
2. Ibid., p. 98.
3. Charles R. Swindoll, *Growing Strong in the Seasons of Life* (Portland, OR: Multnomah Press, 1983), p. 83.
4. Grant, *Being a Woman*, p. 46.
5. Brenda Hunter, *Where Have All the Mothers Gone* (Grand Rapids, MI: Zondervan, 1982), pp. 108-111.
6. Ibid.
7. Fulghum, *All I Really Need,* pp. 17-18.

Chapter Six
1. Grant, *Being a Woman*, pp. 68-69.
2. Willard F. Harley, Jr., *His Needs, Her Needs* (Tarrytown, NY: Fleming H. Revell, 1986), p. 10.
3. Ibid., p. 78.
4. These instructions are based on a detailed model from Harley, *His Needs, Her Needs*, pp. 130-135.

Chapter Seven
1. Joyce Brothers, *What Every Woman Should Know about Men* (New York: Ballantine Books, 1981), p. 31.
2. Doreen Kimura, "Male Brain, Female Brain: The Hidden Difference," *Psychology Today,* Nov. 1985, p. 56.
3. William and Nancy Carmichael with Dr. Timothy Boyd, *That Man! Understanding the Difference between You and Your Husband* (Nashville, TN: Thomas Nelson, 1988), adapted from chapter 2.
4. Warren Farrell, *Why Men Are the Way They Are* (New York: McGraw-Hill, 1986), adapted from p. 139.
5. Carol Gilligan, *In a Different World* (Cambridge, MA: Harvard University Press, 1981), p. 8.
6. Mary Conroy, "Sexism in Our Schools: Training Girls for Failure?" *Better Homes and Gardens,* Feb. 1988, pp. 44-48.
7. Carmichael, Carmichael, and Boyd, *That Man!* adapted from chapter 4.

Chapter Eight

1. Tim Timmons, "Maximum Lifestyle" seminar, Riverside Community Church, Riverside, CA., Mar. 1984.
2. Larry Crabb, *The Marriage Builder* (Grand Rapids, MI: Zondervan, 1982), p. 22.
3. Florence Littauer, *After Every Wedding Comes a Marriage* (Eugene, OR: Harvest House, 1981), p. 22.
4. Fred and Florence Littauer, Freeing Your Mind from the Memories That Bind (San Bernadino, CA: Here's Life Publishers, 1988), pp. 27-30. Additional printed test sheets can be ordered from CLASS Speakers, 1645 South Rancho Santa Fe Road, San Marcos, California 92069.
5. Florence Littauer, Personalities in Power (Lafayette, LA: Huntington House, 1989), pp. 20-32.

Chapter Nine

1. Colleen and Louis Evans, Jr., *My Lover, My Friend* (Old Tappan, NJ: Fleming H. Revell, 1976), pp. 121-123.
2. Hybels, *Honest to God*, points adapted from pp. 101-104.
3. Alan Loy McGinnis, *The Friendship Factor* (Minneapolis, MN: Augsburg, 1979), p. 23.
4. Ibid., p. 9.
5. Jerry and Barbara Cook, *Choosing to Love* (Ventura, CA: Regal Books, 1982), pp. 78-80.

Chapter Ten

1. Marion Woodman, *Addiction to Perfection: The Unravished Bride* (Toronto: Inner City Books, 1982), page 7.
2. Grant, *Being a Woman*, summarized from pp. 88-89.
3. Cook and Cook, *Choosing to Love*, pp. 18-19.
4. Wright, *Quiet Times for Couples*, p. 339.
5. Ibid., p. 100.

Chapter Eleven

1. Harold J. Sala, *Today Can Be Different* (Ventura, CA: Regal Books, 1988), part of the devotional for July 6.

Chapter Twelve

1. *Los Angeles Times*, June 19, 1991.
2. Littauer and Littauer, *Freeing Your Mind*, adapted from pp. 31-35.

3. Patrick Morley, *The Man in the Mirror* (Brentwood, TN: Wolgemuth & Hyatt, 1989), p. 78.
4. Hybels, *Honest to God*, p. 136.
5. Wright, *Quiet Times for Couples*, p. 57.
6. Donald R. Harvey, *The Drifting Marriage* (Old Tappan, NJ: Fleming H. Revell, 1988), p. 99.
7. Wirt and Beckstrom, *Topical Encyclopedia*, p. 259.

Chapter Thirteen
1. Hybels, *Honest to God*, p. 31.
2. Grant, *Being a Woman*, pp. 96-97.
3. Ibid., p. 98.
4. Roy Croft in Joan Winmill Brown and Bill Brown, *Together Each Day* (Old Tappan, NJ: Fleming H. Revell, 1940), p. 43.
5. Wright, *Quiet Times for Couples* p. 357.
6. Barnes and Barnes, *Growing a Great Marriage* , p. 22.
7. Florida Scott-Maxwell, *Women and Sometimes Men* (New York: Alfred A. Knopf, 1957), p. 47.
8. Gordon Dalbey, *Healing the Masculine Soul* (Waco, TX: Word Books, 1988), p. 53.
9. Source unknown.

Chapter Fourteen
1. Rainey and Rainey, *Building Your Mate's Self-Esteem*, adapted from p. 212.
2. Wright, *Quiet Time for Couples*, p. 18.
3. Advice from marriage counselors Samuel and Esther King who appeared on Don McNeil's "Breakfast Club," 1951.

Other Good Harvest House Reading

QUIET TIMES FOR COUPLES
by *H. Norman Wright*

Noted counselor and author Norm Wright provides the help you need to nurture your oneness in Christ. In a few moments together each day you will discover a deeper, richer intimacy with each other and with God, sharing your fondest dreams and deepest thoughts—creating memories of quiet times together.

MORE HOURS IN MY DAY
by *Emilie Barnes*

There can be more hours in your day when you use the collection of calendars, charts, and guides in this useful book on home time management.

THE CREATIVE HOME ORGANIZER
by *Emilie Barnes*

Most of the stress we experience is caused by a lack of organization and can be eliminated with careful planning and timely tips. Bursting with fast and easy methods to save time and energy in your home, *The Creative Home Organizer* has helpful hints for every area of your home. You can learn how to manage a household economically and have fun while doing it! Emilie Barnes also authored *More Hours in My Day* and *Survival for Busy Women.*

SURVIVAL FOR BUSY WOMEN
Establishing Efficient Home Management
by *Emilie Barnes*

A hands-on manual for establishing a more efficient home-management program. Over 25 charts and forms can be personalized to help you organize your home.

THE 15-MINUTE MONEY MANAGER
by *Bob & Emilie Barnes*

At last, a money-management book for busy people! Watch your finances come into focus as you apply the author's proven 15-minute principle: Invest a small amount of time and make a big difference. Sixty-two short, quick-reading chapters have hundreds of ready-to-use ideas that will help you manage your money.

THE 15-MINUTE ORGANIZER
by *Emilie Barnes*

The 15-Minute Organizer is a dream book for the hurried and harried. Its 80 chapters are short and direct so you get right to the answers you need that will let you get ahead and stay ahead when the demands of life threaten to pull you behind.

THE COMPLETE HOLIDAY ORGANIZER
by *Emilie Barnes*

The busy woman's answer to holiday planning, *The Complete Holiday Organizer* gives ideas and helpful hints to make celebration preparations easier. A brief history about each holiday will challenge you to begin your own family traditions and memories. A practical "how-to" book to help you get a handle on holiday organization.

Dear Reader:

We would appreciate hearing from you regarding this Harvest House nonfiction book. It will enable us to continue to give you the best in Christian publishing.

1. What most influenced you to purchase *Your Husband Your Friend*?
   - ☐ Author
   - ☐ Subject matter
   - ☐ Backcover copy
   - ☐ Recommendations
   - ☐ Cover/Title
   - ☐ _____

2. Where did you purchase this book?
   - ☐ Christian bookstore
   - ☐ General bookstore
   - ☐ Department store
   - ☐ Grocery store
   - ☐ Other

3. Your overall rating of this book:
   - ☐ Excellent ☐ Very good ☐ Good ☐ Fair ☐ Poor

4. How likely would you be to purchase other books by this author?
   - ☐ Very likely
   - ☐ Somewhat likely
   - ☐ Not very likely
   - ☐ Not at all

5. What types of books most interest you? (check all that apply)
   - ☐ Women's Books
   - ☐ Marriage Books
   - ☐ Current Issues
   - ☐ Self Help/Psychology
   - ☐ Bible Studies
   - ☐ Fiction
   - ☐ Biographies
   - ☐ Children's Books
   - ☐ Youth Books
   - ☐ Other _____

6. Please check the box next to your age group.
   - ☐ Under 18
   - ☐ 18-24
   - ☐ 25-34
   - ☐ 35-44
   - ☐ 45-54
   - ☐ 55 and over

Mail to: Editorial Director
Harvest House Publishers
1075 Arrowsmith
Eugene, OR 97402

Name _____

Address _____

City _____ State _____ Zip _____

**Thank you for helping us to help you
in future publications!**